THE MISSING PEACE

THE MISSING PEACE

LES CARTER

MOODY PRESS

CHICAGO

All Scripture quotations, unless noted otherwise, are from the *Holy Bible: New International Version.* Copyright © 1973, 1978, 1984 by the International Bible Society. Used by permission of Zondervan Bible Publishers.

Library of Congress Cataloging in Publication Data

Carter, Les.
    The missing peace / by Les Carter.
        p.   cm.
    ISBN 0-8024-5153-5
    1. Peace of mind—Christianity.   I. Title.
    BV4908.5.C37   1987
    248.8'6—dc19   87-22777
                                                                              CIP

2 3 4 5 6 Printing/ A F /Year 91 90 89 88

Printed in the United States of America

To my father, Ed Carter.
Thank you for your early support
in my professional growth
and your continued stimulation
of my thinking processes.

Contents

Acknowledgments

In the fall of 1979, while practicing at a small counseling clinic in Dallas, I was asked to join the Minirth-Meier clinic staff. I was pleased to become part of the team, having no idea of what God would do with the clinic in the coming years. Frank Minirth, as president, is responsible for the philosophic direction of the clinic, and I am grateful to him for his unwaivering commitment to the Word of God as the ultimate resource in the practice of psychiatry. God has blessed him and Paul Meier as they have dedicated their professional lives to His service, and I am pleased to call them my friends and colleagues.

Since that time, the team has grown from seven doctors to almost fifty counselors and doctors. We have written books expressing our commitment to Christ and have had the opportunity to minister to hundreds of thousands each day through radio and television ministries. I thank God for raising up professionals who are devoted to healing emotional wounds through the redemptive teaching of Christianity.

I also wish to thank many individuals for their influence in my thinking: Ross Banister, Bob Abrahamson, Connie Adler, Gerald Marsh, George Woodruff, Bill Goodin, Dick Meier, Don Hawkins, Steve Cretin, Chris Thurman, Paul Warren, States Skipper, Robert G. Packard, Garry Landreth, my pastor, Bill Weber, and my brother, Lee Carter. And I thank Lynn Spencer for her help in preparing the original manuscript of this book.

Also, I appreciate the counselees I have worked with through the years. Their willingness to be open has been of invaluable assistance in my understanding of human nature.

Part 1

Discovering and Understanding Who We Are

ONE
INNER PEACE IS NOT AUTOMATIC

After a deep sigh, Charles said, "I honestly don't know what to do with myself. I've been a Christian since my teen years. You'd think I'd have it together by now. But just when I start feeling good about myself, I have an emotional outburst, and then I feel guilty and depressed. I'm as erratic now as I've ever been."

I had seen that look of frustration a thousand times before. In fact, it has appeared on my own face. Charles was going through the growing pains of finding peace with himself.

Charles was not ignorant. He knew God's Word commanded him to be an imitator of Christ and to walk in His love. He knew he should pray for God's guidance. He knew he should give God authority over his life. He knew that composure would come as he set aside selfish pursuits, seeking God's will first. Yet in spite his knowledge, he had recurring emotional struggles. Half jokingly Charles stated, "At least I can understand the anguish that prompted Paul to write, 'Wretched man that I am.' He knew what it was like to be on an inward roller coaster—well-intended in thought but imperfect in life-style."

Indeed, the apostle Paul's cry in Romans 7 is one that each of us can identify with. Like Paul, we wish to do what is right, but our resulting actions are not what we desire. That fact can explain why so many Christians have struggles with depression, worry, fear, and anger. Not one of us can attain wholeness on our own effort. It is impossible.

Yet Jesus Himself said, "My peace I leave with you." Believers can claim that promise. Philippians 4:11 records the testimony of Paul, who discovered inner composure in spite of his natural predisposition toward sin: "I have learned to be content in whatever circumstance I am." Paul learned that it is possible to find God's peace. A sinner does not have to remain in bondage to his emotions.

THE AGENT OF CHANGE

Jesus gives believers the capacity to make peace with their emotions. God has given each believer a tool, which, when properly utilized, can become an agent of change. That tool is the mind. More specifically, it is the mind fixed on the inerrant Word of God.

Our lives are governed by our mental processes. Each day our minds entertain thousands of thoughts that give direction to every emotion, communication, and behavior. Operating on both a conscious and subconscious level, our minds are the central control bases of our beings. Therefore, the way we choose to use our minds' powers directly affects the quality of our lives.

Consider these facts. The mind distinguishes 300,000 auditory tones and 10,000 odors. It perceives objects both a few millimeters and many light years away. It regulates motor activities such as walking, throwing a ball, and driving a car. It contains hundreds of thousands of thoughts on a range of subjects, from religion, sports, and geography to literature and family secrets. Its powers are unimaginable and beyond human comprehension.

Yet as powerful as the mind is, there is another force that is capable of thwarting it—the power of sin. Sin causes the mind to produce hundreds of negative thoughts every day. Sin can prompt us to indulge in emotions that are both painful and destructive. Above all, sin tempts us to interact with the world in ways that bring disastrous results.

Indwelling sin creates sexual struggles by causing the mind to indulge in lustful thoughts. Sin causes feelings of impatience and irritability. Sin is at the root of thoughtlessness and forgetfulness and at the heart of every insensitive, critical statement. The power of sin permeates every aspect of our mental processes.

Although the mind is powerful, when driven by the forces of sin it can turn a life into a shambles. No wonder the Bible gives special attention to the role of our minds in our quest for peace. Scripture reminds us that we can submit to the will of God only when we focus our minds on godly things:

> The steadfast of mind Thou wilt keep in perfect peace. (Isaiah 26:3)

> As he thinks within himself, so is he. (Proverbs 23:7)

> Walk no longer just as the Gentiles also walk, in the futility of their mind. (Ephesians 4:17)

> Whatever is true, whatever is honorable, whatever is right, whatever is pure, whatever is lovely, whatever is of good repute, if there is anything excellent and if anything worthy of praise, let your mind dwell on these things. (Philippians 4:8)

> For the mind set on the flesh is death, but the mind set on the Spirit is life and peace. (Romans 8:6)

Those verses imply that each individual can make deliberate choices about what thoughts and emotions are given prominence. We may not always be able to determine which thoughts and emotions will appear on our mental screens, but we do have the ability to choose what we will do with those that do appear. We can yield to sin, wallowing in self-absorbed thoughts and emotions, or we can yield to the direction of the Holy Spirit.

It may seem simplistic to break down our foundation for living into mental choices. Yet close analysis of personality reveals that the mind precedes every behavior, emotion, and communication. The choices of the mind fuel our lives just as pressure on an accelerator fuels a car. We may choose either the mind-set of sin or the mind-set of the Holy Spirit.

The key to emotional balance is summarized in Romans 12:2: "Do not be conformed to this world, but *be transformed by the renewing of your minds"* (emphasis added). Individuals who seek a change in their lives have sometimes already consulted God's Word, read books, or sought advice from friends and family members. But often they are still frustrated in their search for peace.

According to Romans 12:2, an individual's life will not be significantly changed without a renewing of the mind. Mental renewal requires more than reading Scripture and dwelling on positive thoughts—although those activities are helpful. Peace with our emotions will come only when we understand the thoughts that guide our emotions. Then we must seek Christ's empowerment and guidance in all areas of thinking and yield ourselves to Him. Such understanding will lead to changes in our relationships with God, family, and friends.

There are three major components in making peace with our emotions.

SEARCHING AND DISCOVERING

In the pursuit of personal transformation, an inquisitive mind is a tremendous asset. An inquisitive mind is not afraid to ask difficult questions. Before outward solutions can be found, inward thoughts, opinions, and philosophies must be clearly described.

Recently a young man noticed on my desk a book detailing Islamic customs. He asked why I bothered to read such material. I replied that my mind was challenged when I read books on a wide variety of subjects and that those new ideas helped me understand why I believed as I did. The young man was dismayed by my answer. He told me that he didn't want to think through his philosophies on a deep level. He said, "Just tell me what I'm supposed to do at work and at home, and I'll be satisfied."

Our lives will have little substance as long as we choose not to search. We cannot expect to be told what to do. Responsible living requires more than a list of dos and don'ts.

We must be willing to face our emotional struggles and seek the underlying thoughts that produce them.

The process of searching and discovering is ongoing. I counseled one man who stated, "The more I discover about myself, the more I realize that there is so much more to discover!"

UNDERSTANDING

Discovering the factors behind our emotions helps us understand ourselves. Self-understanding includes familiarity with our emotional needs, behavior, and human nature. It requires insight and discernment regarding the thoughts and ideas that influence emotions and behavior.

As one who was taught the virtues of Christian living early, I have known the validity of a life of godly love, kindness, and joy for as long as I can remember. But during my early adult years, I was often deficient in those traits. My competitive nature was a stumbling block to me. Although competitiveness propelled me toward various achievements—such as the completion of graduate school—it also created such traits as impatience, stubbornness, and criticalness.

As I sought to understand why I had become so competitive, I found many answers. One was that I was a twin who for years had been compared with my brother. In whatever area I performed, I received comparisons: "Hey, you really showed up your brother that time!" "What are you going to do if your brother beats you in this?" I heard those types of statements so often that I became sensitive toward evaluation.

When I understood how my experiences with competitiveness influenced my thoughts, I modified my mental processes so that I became less sensitive to others' judgments. Understanding myself in that area did not guarantee that I would change, but it played a key role in the mental renewal that led to a deeper desire for God's direction in my life.

When we understand why we struggle, we can better focus on the God-pleasing thoughts that will bring contentment. Self-understanding leads to the third and most vital aspect of finding emotional peace.

YIELDING

Gaining insight about and understanding of ourselves is a humbling experience. For some it is overwhelming. One woman said, "I'm not sure I like the reality of what I'm learning about myself." As we identify areas that need transformation, and as we understand our feelings, we may come to the conclusion, "If my life is to become orderly, it's going to take a power stronger than me."

This much is certain: if we are ever to live consistently we must set aside self's sinful tendencies and yield our minds to the leadership of the Holy Spirit. The most important element in our search for peace is knowing how to yield our minds to God. Mental yielding is defined as voluntary surrender of our rights to God. When we yield our minds to the will of God we become eager to know God's preferences. We will hunger for His Word, seek time for prayer and contemplation, and become attuned to the guidance of the Holy Spirit.

One man who spent years studying the Bible and reading books about Christian living was able to identify weaknesses in his personality. He even knew how he had developed those traits. But in spite of his pursuit of intellectual understanding, his emotional problems persisted. After eight years of study, he focused on Galatians 2:20: "I have been crucified with Christ; and it is no longer I who live, but Christ lives in me." He had read that verse many times before, but this time the phrase "it is no longer I who live" leaped off the page. And as he pondered why he had not experienced transformation before, he discovered the key. He said, "I've gained deep insights about myself, and I've formulated good plans for my future behavior, but I sought to implement those plans myself. I'm not going to find peace until I learn to consider myself crucified and let Christ live in me." He realized that transformation could not take place as long as he was in control. He finally was able to change when he set aside self's efforts, declaring, "Lord, my mind is yours, and I will do as you lead me."

Although making peace with our emotions requires honest self-appraisal and an understanding of our deepest thoughts, the process is not complete until we allow the Holy Spirit to empower us.

WHY CHRISTIANS HAVE EMOTIONAL TURMOIL

Some people ask me, "Shouldn't Christians acquire inner peace from their salvation experience?" They believe that Christianity has all the answers to life's questions and that "real" Christians shouldn't have the struggles that plague the secular world. In fact, they believe that if a Christian gets to the point of needing psychotherapy, he must *really* have a poor relationship with God. Such people assume that if Christians would just do as the Bible commands, their problems would be solved.

Recently I received a phone call from a man who echoed those very thoughts as he spoke about his adult daughter's decision to seek counseling. He feared that his daughter (who was a believer) was a weaker person for having sought therapy, and he feared that she might be led astray by liberal pop-philosophical reasoning. "Don't you think Christian counseling is just a waste?" he asked. "Why can't Christians just read the Bible and do what it tells them to do?"

That man's questions are understandable. And since much of modern psychology *is* based on ungodly reasoning, his thinking reflects a certain amount of truth. Yet at the same time, such thinking is idealistic. Furthermore, although concerns about liberal philosophies of life are legitimate, they are too generalized. Not all therapists ascribe to a "live and let live" philosophy. Some counselors *do* believe in the inerrancy of God's Word.

Christians *should* look to Scripture for guidance. They *should* be one step ahead of the world in the pursuit of inner peace. God's Word *is* the perfect blueprint for living, and if closely followed, it *does* produce genuine composure. But we do not live in an ideal world. Christians are not ideal people. In fact, some people who call themselves Christians are not Christians at all.

Each of our personalities is a mixed bag of experiences, traits, and tendencies. Some people have a powerful blend of spiritual and psychological insights that enable them to handle life's difficulties with ease. Others, however, have a more fragile mixture of experiences that make them vulnerable to emotional stress and interpersonal insecurities. They are not ungodly simply because they need help. They are merely trying to make sense out of their confusing lives.

With that in mind, we'll examine several factors that explain why Christians do not always experience perfect peace.

1. *The secular world encourages a humanistic foundation for living.* No matter how much we are exposed to Christian philosophy, we are still vulnerable to a "me first" attitude. The world bombards us with messages that encourage sensuality, greed, and aggressive anger. We all know people who have succumbed to self-gratifying temptations. And the more we witness the self-seeking pursuits of others, the more we rationalize the same for ourselves. Repeated exposure to others' worldliness can change our sense of morality. For example, Christians currently have a higher tendency toward extramarital affairs than they did ten years ago. Our minds have become so numbed to humanistic philosophy that, over time, many Christians find themselves watering down God's absolutes.

2. *We struggle inwardly with the sin nature.* Since the day Satan enticed Adam and Eve to rebel against God, sin has been rampant. No one is immune. It would be fantastic if we could end our problem with sin by becoming Christians. Some people even assume that will happen. But even godly people experience an inward tug of war (see Romans 7:15). This struggle with sin can eventually wear us down. It can create problems of loneliness, depression, marital discord, and sexual frustration. Some people even reach the point of suicide. They feel so defeated by sin that death seems to be the only way out. They have become entrenched in a pattern of defeat.

3. *Some come from an unstable family background that has taught them bad habits.* God created the family as an illus-

tration of His love for us. In many families, however, that concept is lost. God created the role of the father to teach His followers about His own fatherly love. But how many fathers are aware that their position carries such a strong responsibility? Unfortunately, very few.

Some children are reared in homes where love is not expressed well. Insecurities result, anger and rebellion build, and needs go unmet. As those children grow into adulthood, their problems become so deeply ingrained that they need guidance in order to develop new, healthy habits. And learning new ways of relating can be as difficult and time-consuming as learning to speak a new language.

4. *Most adults lack training in the two most important responsibilities of life—marriage and parenting.* In my seminars, I often mention that in Texas it takes four years of extensive training to get an electrician's license but only four minutes to apply for a marriage license!

Many people who appear to have normal, healthy personalities admit that they are able to get along well with almost anyone except their spouse and kids. They are not devoid of personal skills, but usually they have had little or no training in the intricacies of family communications. No one taught them how to handle emotions such as anger, impatience, or worry. And no one encouraged them to examine their philosophy of communication. As a result, they find family life overwhelming and bewildering.

5. *We live in a high stress society.* The world pressures us to perform. From the time we begin school to the day we retire, judgmental eyes are fixed on us, watching every achievement, making evaluations at every turn. As a result, it is easy to become sidetracked mentally and emotionally by the opinions and concerns of others. We can become so concerned about our standing with others that we lose sight of the importance of our standing with God. Rather than looking to him for emotional composure, we look first to our human judges. Having become mentally caught in the performance trap of our highly competitive world, we can be brought to our knees in stress, false hopes, and frustrations.

6. *Most of us have minimal insight into how faith in God can change our lives.* Almost daily I talk to people who know the important truths of Scripture but who find it almost impossible to be helped by those truths. I am reminded of a man who was as proficient at Bible memorization as anyone I've met. He probably knew more Scripture and doctrine than 99 percent of average church members. Yet he was involved in repeated sexual affairs and was prone to terrible temper outbursts. What was wrong? We discovered that although he had memorized many biblical truths, he was blind to some serious problems in his personality (particulary his self-image). Though he wanted to apply his faith, his inner struggles continued to plague him. His psychological problems hindered his ability to integrate his biblical knowledge into his life. Sometimes we must first understand our inner anger, loneliness, unresolved guilt, and other emotional baggage before we can appropriate God's truth. But most of us are untrained in such matters.

None of us is immune to problems. In fact, a large percentage of us experiences tremendous turbulence during the problems of life. That is why we must come to terms with our emotional selves.

This book is intended to help us do that. First we will search the Scripture for what it says about mankind and what he can be. We will then explore how to yield our mental processes in ways that lead us to emotional peace. Finally, we will examine ways of conforming our life-style to the Person of Christ.

TWO
THE ORIGIN OF EMOTIONAL STRUGGLES

We all share common, predictable emotions. The negative aspects of those emotions result from man's fall into sin. Peace comes only when we uncover and understand the underlying thoughts and beliefs that guide our emotions. But those guiding thoughts are often subconscious, and we must use an indirect route to discern them. We must first identify and understand the emotions that are basic to our human nature.

Once discovered, our emotions can keep us honest about what lies within our minds. So in a sense, our emotions provide an open window to our guiding thoughts. Emotional struggles can serve as a warning flag to problems in our deepest attitudes and guiding beliefs. The writer of Proverbs tells us that as we think within ourselves, so we are (23:7). And the best way to examine the thoughts that influence our behaviors is by discovering and understanding our emotional tendencies.

Recently I spoke with a husband who stated that he was a self-confident man, free from insecurity. Yet he had a problem with anger and was often critical and bossy. As we explored the meaning of his anger, we found that the excessive anger was linked to the fear of being dominated—a fear that originated in childhood. Furthermore, anger occurred when he became snared in hidden feelings of inferiority, which he masked with the drive to become superior. We also discovered that his emotions spoke of problems in other areas, such as a fear of loving, feelings of loneliness and isolation, and needless defensiveness. Identifying the underlying contributors to his anger helped uncover his real self. Only through a thorough analysis of the thoughts behind his emotions was he able to honestly confront the underlying beliefs that influenced his behavior.

Understanding our common emotions is the first step in comprehending our guiding thoughts. Now we arrive at a second critical point: no emotion can be understood singularly and apart from the other emotions. Our emotional experiences are linked in a cause-and-effect chain.

In an attempt to understand an emotion (such as worry or envy), laypersons and professionals alike often make the mistake of isolating one problem and trying to explain it as a distinct issue. For example, in trying to solve a case of depression, one may be tempted to focus only on the issue of sadness. "Why are you so sad?" "What have other people done to create this sadness in you?" "What do you think you could do to make yourself feel better?" Those questions in and of themselves are fine. They cause one to think about some of the origins of the emotion. But they don't go far enough.

To understand that depression is not isolated from other emotions, consider the role of anger in depression. Listen to the words of a depressed person, and you can easily detect an undertow of repressed anger. "I hate the way my mother treats me." "Life just isn't fair." "Who cares anymore?" An understanding of a person's depression is improved through an understanding of his anger.

But it doesn't stop there. Consider some of the other emotions that are linked to depression, such as inferiority or false guilt. A person may be harboring feelings of lowered self-esteem. What about loneliness? Depression can be triggered by a nagging feeling of emptiness and isolation from loved ones. What about fear? Defensiveness? Pride? Those emotional issues can be direct contributors to depression. And each underlying feeling can communicate more about the subconscious beliefs and thought patterns that directly influence our quality of life. In order to understand a single emotion, we must first be aware of the interaction between our emotions.

Like a chain, our emotions are linked to each other inexorably, and one emotional response is either the source or the result of others.

THE FIVE BASIC EMOTIONAL STRUGGLES

We have made two major assumptions: (1) understanding our basic emotional struggles requires an honest appraisal of our underlying thoughts and beliefs, and (2) a single emotion must be understood not as a separate phenomenon but as part of a whole.

The Bible offers information useful for understanding the origins of mankind's basic struggles. In order to gain a full view of our emotional selves, therefore, we must start at the beginning of the biblical record, where all problems originated.

In the Genesis account of mankind's fall into sin, we see a snowball effect—one emotional problem led to another, then another, then another. As we understand what each of these emotional problems communicates, we begin to get a clear picture of our own mental processes.

Keep in mind that the story of Adam and Eve is the story of you and me. What they experienced is representative of what we experience. Although their situation occurred thousands of years ago, human nature is still the same.

All emotional problems can be traced through five basic emotions. As we examine these emotions, keep in mind that they are listed in an order of progression; that is, the first emotion has a direct bearing on the second emotion, which directly influences the third emotion, and so on. We cannot completely understand our emotional selves until we come to terms with the interaction of these emotions.

PRIDE

Picture life in the Garden of Eden in the days before sin. Communication between Adam and Eve was complete. Their minds were perfectly attuned to purity of thought. They had no emotional struggles; empathy was present in all their interactions. They had a perfect understanding of one another's feelings and needs, and they shared continuous joy and laughter. The happiness they experienced came in direct correlation to their personal relationship with God.

We could use the word *proud* to summarize the way Adam and Eve felt about themselves. By that I mean that they felt a deep and abiding sense of pleasure and satisfaction with the life God had given them. And they maintained a positive regard and enthusiasm about who they were and about life in general. God desired that they experience His joy to the fullest.

In his effort to gain dominion over Adam and Eve, Satan chose to attack this beneficial aspect of pride. He appealed first to Eve's pride and then Adam's, creating a desire for self-worship by drawing them away from God and into themselves. Sinful pride is clearly the first and foremost of all emotional problems. God's gift to Adam and Eve became twisted.

> Now the serpent was more crafty than any beast of the field which the Lord God had made. And he said to the woman, "Indeed, has God said, 'You shall not eat from any tree of the garden'?" And the woman said to the serpent, "From the fruit of the trees of the garden we may eat; but from the fruit of the tree which is in the middle of the garden, God has said, 'You shall not eat from it or touch it, lest you die.' " And the serpent said to the woman, "You surely shall not die! For God knows that in the day you eat from it your eyes will be opened and you will be like God, knowing good and evil." (Genesis 3:1-5)

Eve was without blemish. She had a high sense of importance and self-esteem. Recall a time in your own life when you had an extra bounce in your gait, hummed an upbeat tune, and reached out to another with a friendly hello and a pat on the back. At such times you knew an inward glow that made you say, "All is well. I'm pleased with life." Now imagine what it would be like to feel that way every minute of the day, every day of the week. That's what life was like for Eve. She didn't just have a taste of the good life; she had it all.

Satan always looks for a way to gain an advantage, even when the odds seem unrealistically stacked against him. Satan thought, *I'll try to get Eve to feel dissatisfied about who she is and what she has with God. I'll entice her to crave a greater sense of self-importance.* Satan threw out the bait, in effect saying, "Eve, how would you like to be like God? How would you like to make yourself the center of the universe? If you think life is grand now, just imagine how much better it could be if you called all the shots."

In essence, Satan's temptation caused Eve to carry her desire for satisfaction with life to the extreme and to become completely absorbed with her own thoughts about how life ought to proceed. That's what sinful pride does. Sinful pride is defined as a feeling of preoccupation with self's needs, desires, and importance. It is an overconcern with self and a need to control circumstances (as opposed to allowing God to control our lives). So when Eve succumbed to Satan's temptation she in effect thought, *Hey, wouldn't it be great to be a god! Maybe then I could do things my way. The world would cater to me!*

With Eve's fateful decision to put self first, sinful pride came into being. The positive feeling of pride that Adam and Eve experienced turned into selfish desire. And since sinful pride is the original emotion of mankind's Fall, we can surmise that it is at the foundation of all emotional struggles. Whether an individual is prone to overt displays (such as shouting or whining) or covert expressions (such as holding grudges or withdrawing), pride is at the base. Examine a broad array of problems and you will find that resentment, arrogance, hostile anger, envy, jealousy, defensiveness, oversensitivity, depression, inferiority, false guilt, infatuated love, and even loneliness all have pride at the core. An understanding of any other emotional problem will be incomplete without an understanding of pride.

Consider selfishness in young children. Before a child has even a chance to become self-absorbed, this trait appears. When playing with other toddlers, an eighteen-month-old child is concerned with himself. Sharing must be taught and reinforced. Grabbing and whining are behaviors that no one ever teaches a child. They are innate.

As a child progresses through elementary, junior high, and high school, selfish tendencies remain. Fueled by competitiveness, a need for approval, and a desire for self-satisfaction, sinful pride remains firmly entrenched. The only difference between one individual and the next is the means by which pride is manifested. It becomes the task of each adult to come to terms with his own pride, recognizing the influence it has on his life.

Recognizing that sinful pride involves preoccupation with self, let's go one step further and examine the thoughts that underlie this emotion.

A person who harbors sinful pride is likely to entertain such thoughts as:

- I'll be pleased with life when things go according to my expectations.
- I really believe that I know what is best. You can't tell me anything new.
- I think it is ridiculous when people don't agree with me.
- Maybe it's true that God should be first in my life, but I really feel a need to be in control.
- It's much easier to love and accept people when they agree with me.
- I think people should think highly of me, or at least show me a great deal of respect.
- I'll feel much more comfortable with my life when I gain more influence over my surroundings.

Sinful pride is at the bottom of each emotional problem we encounter. No emotional difficulty can be resolved until the problem of pride is properly addressed.

FEAR

After improper pride was introduced in mankind's fall into sin, fear was the next emotional experience. As Adam and Eve defied God in their sinful pride, their eyes were opened to the severity of their decision:

And they heard the sound of the Lord God walking in the garden in the cool of the day, and the man and his wife hid themselves from the presence of the Lord God among the trees of the garden. . . . And [the man] said, "I heard the sound of Thee in the Garden, and I was afraid because I was naked; so I hid myself." (Genesis 3:8, 10)

Adam and Eve experienced a startling turn of events. Having indulged their desire for self-importance, they soon realized that they weren't equipped to handle their new position, and they became fearful. Their decision had not been a good one; they were unable to fulfill the task of being a god. As they felt the first repercussions of their inability to function without God's guidance, apprehension washed over them.

Today we have the same fears. Because we are sinners who through pride have made wrong decisions, we are each prone to fear. No one is exempt, even the one who seems self-reliant. This sense of fear may be obvious in one who is indecisive, doubtful, or prone to phobias. Or it may be more subtle in one who is defensive, phony, or unwilling to admit personal flaws.

The level of fear in our lives is proportional to the level of sinful pride. The more self-absorbed we are, the more apprehensive we are about the approval or rejection of our peers. Undue fear speaks volumes about our preoccupation with self. It also reveals the prideful need to be in a god-like position of control, "calling the shots" according to self's dictates.

A man who feels a need to be treated with dignity and respect may tell himself that he *must* be given special treatment by his wife when he arrives home from work. If his wife is not in the best of moods when he arrives home, a subtle fear appears. On the surface he may exhibit irritability, but beneath the surface he is thinking, *Oh, no, she's not treating me in the grand fashion that I had hoped for. I can't handle it. What will I do?* The fear may be so subtle that he does not identify it; nonetheless, it is there and at work.

To further understand our natural inclination toward fear, let's examine some experiences common to children.

Children can be frightened by such things as a loud noise, a harsh rebuke, a new circumstance, or a dark room. As children grow older, simpler fears begin to subside, but a remnant remains. Although adults may not be fearful of such things as crawling bugs or shrill sounds, they are fearful of abstract things such as rejection, loss of status, or condescending communication from others. Like pride, fear is a natural and predictable emotion. The only difference between one person and the next is the substance and degree of that fear.

Once we recognize the presence of fear in each of us, we can analyze the thoughts that are associated with fear. As is the case with all emotions, fear can shed light on the true beliefs that motivate our outward behaviors. Fear is indicated through thoughts such as:

- I don't feel secure about who I am.
- I assume that people can't be trusted with my self-disclosures.
- I can't allow people to see the *real* me.
- I won't be able to handle it if my circumstances go counter to my desires.
- I have doubts about the decisions that I have made.

Do you see a snowball effect beginning? First man was enticed to think more highly of himself than was warranted; he elevated himself to the position reserved for God. The result was a warped sense of sinful pride, preoccupation with self, and insecurity. Because we were not created to be gods, we each have an underlying apprehension about our position in life. That apprehension leads directly to the next of the five basic emotions—loneliness.

LONELINESS

Once mankind fell into indulgent pride, leading to fear and apprehension, a third basic emotional problem developed—the problem of loneliness. Simply defined, loneliness is a feeling of separation, emptiness, and alienation from God and others. It can even be felt in a sense of estrangement from oneself, as in the case of the person who says, "I'm not even sure I know myself."

Adam and Eve hid themselves from God in fear: "Then the Lord God called to the man, and said to him, 'Where are you?' " (Genesis 3:9). The perfect fellowship Adam and Eve experienced with God was broken. We can't be sure what form the fellowship between God and man had taken before sin. We don't know if Adam and Eve could see God physically or converse with Him audibly. But we do know that when sin entered their lives, the intimate fellowship they shared with God was lost.

Not only were Adam and Eve separated from God, but they were irreversibly separated from each other. They no longer felt the desire or the ability to be open. Deception had taken the place of perfect trust. Their understanding for each other was lost; their communication became calculated. Even though they were to remain together as partners and lovers, their relationship had taken a giant step downward. They faced feelings of aloneness and isolation that God never desired them to experience (see Genesis 2:18).

Adam and Eve's unhappy plight has been passed to each successive generation. Every person has felt the pain of loneliness. Each of us has experienced the feeling of being disconnected from others. We each have yearned to be touched more intimately, to be comprehended more completely, to be loved more fully. Throughout childhood and into adult life, each person has known some measure of undesirable isolation. No one is immune.

Loneliness can be manifested in a variety of ways. It is present in the one who longs to be loved. It can be seen in the pain of the person who feels a shortage of friendships. Or it can be felt by the one who responds with emptiness to life's offerings. More subtly, it can be felt by the one who feels criticized and condemned. It is at the core of the person who has a "chip on the shoulder" and proclaims that he or she doesn't need people. And it is a motivating force of the one who in infatuation ascribes god-like qualities to another.

Each of us has yearned for more significant interaction and greater understanding between ourself and our loved ones. We admit that our relationships do not achieve perfect unity. In marriage relationships we bemoan communication gaps and differences between personalities. In parent-child relationships we experience the generation gap. At work we feel an adverse atmosphere between management and subordinates. As long as sin is present, loneliness will be present.

As with all emotions, we can look beneath loneliness to the thoughts that direct the behavior. The lonely person harbors such thoughts as:

- People really don't understand me, so what difference does it make?
- Life is futile. I try and try, but I can't get satisfaction.
- My hidden secrets keep me from being as closely connected to others as I would like.
- There is no satisfaction in life if I can't have someone to love me.
- So many people don't know how to relate to me. There's something wrong with me.
- In this world, you have to look out for number one, because no one else will.

The more these thoughts are entertained, the deeper the person falls into the trap of loneliness. As with the other emotions, our mental reactions determine how severely the emotion is experienced.

INFERIORITY

As Adam and Eve began to feel the repercussions of their decision to defy God in sinful pride, they not only felt fear and loneliness, but they lost their high position in the home God had given them. Whereas God's original plan was to give them a glorious life that included a continual relationship of joy with Him, the onset of sin drove them out of their paradise and imposed upon them the consequences of their decision. Their next emotional experience was of inferiority.

Genesis 3:23-24 says, "Therefore, the Lord God sent him out from the garden of Eden, to cultivate the ground from which he was taken. So He drove the man out." Within each of us is the instinctual knowledge that we are not fully what God wants us to be. We do not have what it takes to be perfect. Deep down we know that. Romans 1:20 tells us that God has revealed to every person a knowledge of His divine majesty. And all of us at some level (either conscious or subconscious) know that we cannot possibly measure up to His perfect standard. In fact, God wants us to recognize our inferiority so that we will respond to His invitation to restored fellowship with Him through Jesus Christ.

Most of us respond to our feelings of inferiority in ways that only make it worse. Some individuals, overwhelmed by their sense of inadequacy, develop a cowering, timid nature and assume that they must be resigned to an inferior position. Although we are inferior to Adam's original position of perfection, no sinful human is inferior to another. The people who collapse under the weight of inferiority are likely to develop problems with false guilt, nonassertiveness, shyness, depression, and chronic apologetics.

At the other extreme, some respond to their feelings of inferiority by seeking to make themselves superior. These people assume that if they can gain a competitive edge on someone else—*anyone* else—they will rid themselves of the feeling of unworthiness. Consequently, they go to great lengths to gain the upper hand. They may become overachievers, supercritics, manipulators, braggarts, or snobs. But those behaviors do nothing to resolve their feelings of inferiority. Their striving for superiority only provides them with a temporary feeling of satisfaction, because the problem of inferiority cannot be solved by attaining superiority. Our feeling of inadequacy does not result from our standing with other humans. Mankind's basic inferiority is a consequence of his broken fellowship with God. It will never be resolved until our relationship to Him is restored.

When does this struggle with inferiority begin? When young children explore the world around them (getting into cabinets, playing with forbidden objects, and so on), they soon learn that they are capable of doing things to elicit the displeasure of adults. And as they grow they become aware—often painfully so—that they are unable to perform the same deeds as Mom or Dad. They are dependent on adults to teach them to speak, to drive them to school, to tell them when to go to bed, to tell them when to get up. Even in the most loving homes, a child receives the message "You are not fully adequate." As the years go by, some children learn to put that inadequacy into proper perspective and to avoid comparative evaluations. But there remains the nagging question, "Am I *really* OK?" As long as we are attached to our earthly bodies, we will continue to doubt our self-worth.

The thoughts of a person who feels inferior may include:

- If I don't perform well, it will prove that I am no good.
- When I make a mistake, I'd better have a good explanation for it.
- The Lord may get fed up with me if I don't shape up.
- I'm unable to handle anything that is less than perfect.
- If I fail, my worth as a human drops a notch.

ANGER

The final basic emotion that Adam and Eve experienced as they were driven out of the Garden was anger. Adam and Eve did not take their fall in stride. They harbored feelings of resentment. Going from paradise to a life of toil was not easy to accept. That eventually led them to anger. They wanted to recapture the dignity they had so ignobly lost, but they were frustrated in their efforts. And as they bore children, those children inherited the same emotional problems and began to express their own anger. That is vividly evidenced in Cain's feelings toward his brother Abel:

> And Abel, on his part also brought the firstlings of his flock and of their fat portions. And the Lord had regard for Abel and his offering; but for Cain and his offering He had no regard. So Cain became very angry and his countenance fell. . . . And it came about when they were in the field, that Cain rose up against his brother and killed him. (Genesis 4:4-5, 8)

Finding themselves in the unwanted position of lowered status, Adam and Eve became dissatisfied. That dissatisfaction led to an emotion that primarily advocates self's needs and desires—anger. Notice that the individual who expresses anger is often standing up for his deepest desires. Because the fallen, sinful world offers a guaranteed struggle, this emotion comes about with the need to protect self from perceived wrongs.

As with Cain's anger, our anger is usually misguided by our absorption with self. We can have such a keen awareness of our flaws and inadequacies that we errantly seek to preserve self by striking out against others. Although most of us have not gone as far as Cain did in expressing anger, Jesus Christ made clear that we have the capacity to do so (see Matthew 5:21-22).

No one is immune to anger. Many times in my counseling practice I have heard people say they don't experience anger. But that is not so. Because we each face imperfect, undesirable circumstances, we are confronted with the issue of self-preservation and the accompanying anger. Admittedly, the anger experienced by some people may not be expressed in screaming, cursing, and slamming doors. Consequently, we may avoid the term *anger*, saying instead that we have feelings of frustration or annoyance. But inevitably we have each known moments when we have been unduly critical, sarcastic, bossy, or purposely silent. Because we each have had experiences in which we felt mistreated, spoken condescendingly toward, or misunderstood, we have each felt anger. And because we are all sinners, we will at times express this emotion inappropriately.

No one has to teach a child to cry when he fails to get what he wants. The child knows that screaming and crying can produce self-gratifying results. As we grow older we become more sophisticated in our efforts to take a stand for our wants and beliefs, but anger remains within us as long as we are in the flesh.

Some of the underlying thoughts that motivate individuals as they experience anger are:

- I must stand up for my rights if I'm going to get anything out of my life.
- I absolutely refuse to accept it if someone looks down upon me.
- If anyone treats me badly, I need to get even with them in some way.
- I feel insecure about the fact that people will not take me seriously, so I'd better take a firm stand for myself to prove my strength.
- My needs and my desires are most important.

Keep in mind that the number of instances in which anger is appropriate is small (see Ephesians 4:26). There are times when it is proper to communicate our needs and convictions; however, the majority of our anger is misguided.

THE INTERACTION OF EMOTIONS

Figure 2-1 identifies the five basic emotional struggles and shows how each emotion builds on another. From one end, we see that pride leads to fear, then loneliness, then inferiority, then anger. From another perspective, anger contains elements of inferiority, loneliness, fear, and pride. Each emotion is intricately linked to another in a cause-and-effect relationship.

In figure 2-2, you will notice that many other emotions are related to the five basic emotions. (This listing of emotions is not necessarily exhaustive; more could be included.) We again see that sinful pride is the most basic of emotions and fuels all others. Next to each of the four remaining emotions are listed the feelings most closely related to them.

On the horizontal level, we see that fear can produce doubt, which if fostered can lead to dread. In addition, fear can bring about a defensive cover-up or a psychological resistance to perceived threats. Defensiveness can create problems with phoniness.

Five Basic Emotions

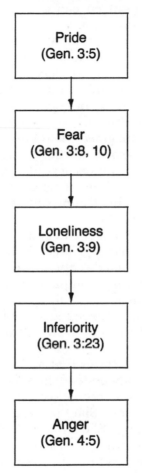

Figure 2-1

Loneliness, with its inherent feelings of emptiness and isolation, yearns for love, attention, and comfort. That yearning, if not properly resolved, can set the individual up for experiences with infatuated love. In addition, loneliness can bring a feeling of lamentation, a sadness that bemoans the fact that life does not offer the rewards we would enjoy. That lamentation can eventually produce grief, a feeling of emptiness due to a loss of something desired and treasured.

The struggle with inferiority can also produce guilt. Guilt can be defined as a feeling of blameworthiness due to offenses committed (real or imagined). This guilt can potentially produce shyness as the individual stays away from experiences that might expose his feelings of guilt and inferiority. In addition, inferiority can spawn deeper feelings of unworthiness and rejection. And as that feeling simmers, it can produce despair and helplessness.

The struggle with anger can easily turn into smoldering resentment, which carries grudges. Left unresolved, depression—a sad and irritated dejection—can result. Likewise, anger can prompt a feeling of impatience when our desires are not quickly met. Impatience can produce worry, which has strong elements of both anger and fear. And worry may either overtly or subtly contribute to struggles with envy and jealousy.

Figure 2-2 demonstrates that no emotion can be experienced (and therefore understood) in isolation from the others.

A woman who is a chronic worrier frets when her children are out of the home. She's uptight whenever she invites company to the house. She's never sure if her husband is pleased with her. Her apprehension about either past or future experiences can readily sap her emotional and physical strength. There is more to worry than just a feeling of apprehension. What key elements does this woman need to address?

Referring to the above figure, we see that several emotions precede worry. Directly preceding worry is a feeling of impatience, which tells us that as a worrier this woman probably has a problem with being too time and duty conscious.

The Interaction of Emotions

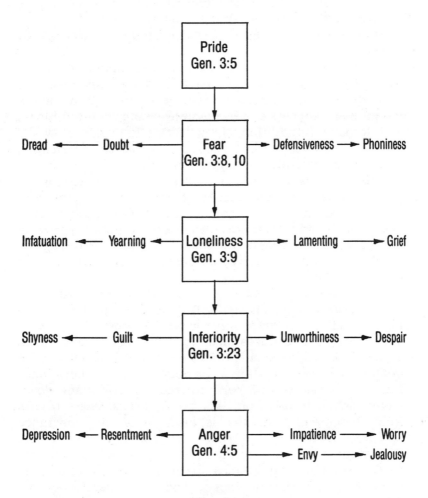

Figure 2-2

In addition, we see that this woman has some underlying problems with anger. So before the worry can be adequately addressed, this woman's problems with anger will need to be exposed and understood. And although resentment and depression are not necessarily direct contributors to worry, they potentially could be.

Proceeding up the list of the five basic emotions, we can see that this woman cannot have a full understanding of self until she uncovers her feelings of inferiority (with its potential guilt and shyness and its possible feeling of unworthiness and despair). In addition, she will have to explore how she handles loneliness (with the possible side issues of yearning, infatuation, lamenting, and grief). She must resolve her fear, and that may expose hidden doubts, unnecessary feelings of defensiveness and phoniness. And then at the foundation of it all, this woman will need to examine her tendencies toward pride. And, to add one more note of caution, since worry is on the same level as anger on the chart, her unresolved struggles with worry can potentially fuel the other emotional spinoffs of anger.

Or consider the case of a man who has problems with chronic defensiveness. He tends to rationalize his flaws, making every effort to expose only the positive side of his personality. His defensiveness can lead to struggles with phoniness. Tracing the origins of this man's defensiveness, we surmise —whether he would admit it or not—that he harbors inner fears, inadequacies, and perhaps traces of doubt and deep-seated dread. In addition, this man's defensiveness results from his sense of pride, that is, his sense of self-importance and preoccupation with himself. The issues of fear and pride, then, would be considered the key elements leading to his defensiveness. Carrying the idea one step further, we could assume that if this man does not deal with his defensiveness, he will eventually experience further problems with loneliness, inferiority, anger, and their accompanying emotional issues.

These illustrations show that we cannot adequately understand a single dimension of our emotions without recognizing its preceding emotional causes and its succeeding emotional ramifications.

THREE
RESOLUTIONS FOR EMOTIONAL STRUGGLES

Each day we are guided by various warnings, many so common that we are hardly aware of them. Most of us begin the day when the alarm clock wakes us. Subconscious messages tell us to be careful as we step into the shower. In traffic, signals tell us when to stop, when to go, when to yield, how fast to travel, and how to avoid road hazards. At work a coworker may give us a knowing look that says, "Beware, the boss is in a bad mood."

We learn to read the faces of loved ones. We know signals that tell us when all is well or when to keep silent. Our bodies give us warnings that alert us to special needs: a yawn signals the need for sleep, and a painful bruise tells us to be more cautious. Warnings such as these are a vital part of life. They help give life order.

In the same way, our emotions are warning signals meant to bring order to life. We have noted that our emotions can be an open window to our inner thoughts, beliefs, and struggles. Emotions are surface symptoms that indicate a need to confront the deeper issues of our mental processes. As we learn to view our troublesome emotions as God's warning system, we can begin to adjust our thought patterns, appealing to God for resolutions.

In the last chapter we identified the five basic emotional struggles, and we noted that all other emotions can be understood in relation to them. As we examined each of those emotions separately, we noticed that each tells us something about the deepest thoughts within the mind. As we identify our own struggles with these emotions and recognize their guiding thoughts, a process of awareness unfolds. Awareness is being alert to and knowledgeable of our deepest personal needs and ideas. Awareness is a vital first step on the road to personal peace. But that awareness raises another issue: What do we do once we become aware of our most basic emotions?

Scott came to my office seeking help for a variety of emotional strains. He had lifelong feelings of inferiority that fueled other emotions such as guilt, unworthiness, passive anger, impatience, and periodic depression. He had been in counseling for more than a year and had not reached the root of his problems. Scott told me, "I've been told what my problems are; I'm not lacking in my knowledge of what needs to be changed. And I've been told what I should do differently. But something's still missing. I don't feel like I have the right tools to make the necessary changes."

Scott's experience is not unlike that of many others who have recurring emotional struggles. He knew what his problems were, and he even knew what some of the answers were, but he was missing the key ingredient. He still needed to discover what his emotions communicated about his guiding thoughts. And he needed to examine biblical truths and integrate new and lasting principles into his mental processes. As he set aside his original guiding thoughts in favor of the timeless truths from God's Word, he was able to make adjustments in his life.

Once we are able to identify our basic emotional struggles and become aware of the thoughts that those emotions represent, we can adjust our lives in light of God's Word. We will examine the five basic principles needed for overcoming emotional struggles. Again, the following principles are presented in progression.

OVERCOMING EMOTIONAL STRUGGLES

SELFLESSNESS

In the last chapter, we noted that mankind's fall into sin originated with sinful pride. Adam and Eve chose to elevate themselves over God. As a result they were left with a nature preoccupied with the importance of self. Preoccupation with self is the beginning of all emotional problems.

Scripture repeatedly instructs us to set aside preoccupation with self in favor of control by God:

> The love of Christ controls us, having concluded this, that one died for all, therefore all died. (2 Corinthians 5:14)

> Consider yourselves to be dead to sin, but alive to God in Christ Jesus. (Romans 6:11)

> Set your mind on the things above, not on the things that are on earth. For you have died and your life is hidden with Christ in God. (Colossians 3:2-3)

> See to it that no one takes you captive through philosophy and empty deception, according to the tradition of man, according to the elementary principles of the world, rather than according to Christ. (Colossians 2:8)

These verses show that a person preoccupation with self's desires is on a collision course with eternal death. The only way to find meaning and purpose in life is to give the direction of our lives to God. That action is summarized in the word *selflessness*. To be selfless means letting go of the desire to control one's world in accordance with self-understanding, choosing to yield to the will of God. Galatians 2:20 vividly captures the concept of selflessness: "I have been crucified with Christ; and it is no longer I who live, but Christ lives in me." As seen in the figure below, that is the antithesis to pride.

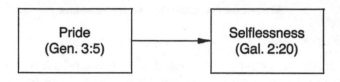

Figure 3-1

Considering the self as crucified is no easy task, and it cannot be done in our own power. The decision to deny self may be made, but the body with all its fleshly lusts and cravings continues to live. The person who decides to deny self predictably steps into a new kind of struggle. It requires daily —even hourly—yielding to God.

Selflessness is summed up in the phrase "I have been crucified with Christ." The death Christ suffered was not just His own death—it was *my* death. When He was buried in the tomb, He represented my sinfulness. And when He was resurrected from the grave, He illustrated the new life that I could have when I trusted Him to be Lord of my life. Christ's death paid the price of sin for all mankind, but its power does not take effect in our lives until we appropriate it individually.

By accepting the substitutionary death of Christ as symbolic of my own death, I recognize that my prideful tendencies can only lead me to destruction. In considering myself crucified, I am stating: "God, my life is no longer mine; it is yours. I submit myself to your counsel and direction, and I let go of my desire to live according to my own knowledge." That does not mean, of course, that I choose not to think, to have opinions, or to make decisions. It means that my life is so saturated in devotion to God that all my thoughts and choices are filtered through a God-controlled mind-set.

Philippians 2:1-11 describes a life of complete service to God. Paul instructs us to consider others more important than ourselves, thus having the same attitude that was in Jesus Christ. Paul then explains that Christ, although He could have exercised His right to be coequal with God, chose to humble Himself by taking the form of a bondslave. Rather than follow the path taken by Adam and Eve, Christ chose to satisfy His heavenly Father. In doing so, He demonstrated His faith in God's ability to uphold Him in every area of need. Though Jesus Christ experienced scorn and anguish as a result of His decision to set self aside, He also embodied love itself. And in the end, God exalted Him, giving Him the ultimate position of glory.

Although we too will experience strains and struggles when we choose to set aside self's preoccupation, God will ultimately bless and exalt us. When His nature indwells us, we can be assured that whatever our circumstances may be, we will be given the pleasure of God's composure and confidence.

It is unnatural for any of us to set aside self in favor of God's leading. From the earliest days of our lives we have desired our own way. Sin has a strong influence over us. That may explain why Christ said, "If anyone wishes to come after me, let him deny himself, and take up his cross daily, and follow me." To live a life pleasing to God, we must begin each day with a new decision to follow Him. If we are not seeking self-denial on a day-by-day basis, we will naturally live according to the ways of sin and the pride of life.

The practice of selflessness is crucial to the resolution of virtually every emotional and relational problem. The married couple experiencing a lack of communication will not resolve their problems until they learn to set aside their preoccupation with self, opting to yield to God's direction. The individual prone to depression from years of repressed anger needs to set aside preoccupation with self and ask God for direction. The person prone to impatience and irritation must set self aside in order to let the traits of the Holy Spirit reside within. Since sinful pride is at the core of all personal struggles, and since selflessness is the direct antithesis of pride, we will never know success in overcoming life's difficulties until we consider ourselves dead to sin.

Carol had suffered a longstanding bout with depression. She would have some good days in which she would feel a normal range of positive and negative emotions, but she could not go more than a week or two without having a couple of days of dark depression where she lacked the motivation to do even the simplest tasks. She had undergone several physical examinations and had been assured that there were no organic origins to her depression.

As Carol talked, many issues other than depression surfaced. Carol felt her marriage offered her less than she originally desired and expected. Communication with her husband wasn't rewarding; their relationship was bland and unstimulating. Also, Carol's two teenagers gave her less respect than she thought she deserved. After all, her life was one of give, give, give. They seemed to show little acknowledgment—let alone appreciation—for her efforts to be a loving mother. Her family background involved mixed interactions. On one hand her parents were prone to dote over her, giving her preferential treatment that made her feel more special than her peers. But at the same time they were demanding, and she felt controlled by them.

In our discussions we discovered that Carol had become disgruntled with life. During a slow—almost imperceivable—progression of time, she had become preoccupied with herself, focusing too heavily on her own wants and desires. Her feelings and desires were not inappropriate; in fact, given her circumstances, a certain measure of those emotions was understandable. However, Carol so keenly focused on herself that she gave a more than healthy prominence to her own ideas of right and wrong. Her depression was communicating, "What about my rights? Notice me. Give me attention!"

Eventually Carol learned to concentrate on one of the key concepts of Scripture—denying self. She learned that denying self did not mean assuming a "doormat" position. Rather it meant letting go of her preoccupation with her own needs long enough to allow God to direct her life. Carol practiced a variety of behaviors such as proper assertion, kindness, servanthood, and forgiveness without preconceived notions regarding the way others should respond. If she was preoccupied with anything, it was not self's needs but the presence of the Lord in her every movement. Paradoxically, Carol learned that when she set self aside, she was most likely to have her deepest needs met.

Just as the presence of pride reveals an individual's innermost guiding thoughts, so does the presence of selflessness. The person who chooses selflessness as a way of life is indulging in such thoughts as:

- I realize that I am not the center of the universe, and I will not demand preferential treatment.
- I know that I do not have the full intellectual ability to successfully control my corner of the world.
- I acknowledge that if I am going to find contentment it will happen as I submit to God.
- The best way for me to have self-control is to decrease my need for controls.
- It is better to be God-conscious than self-conscious.
- Humility is a trait most worthy of pursuit.

As we allow such thoughts to guide us, we can be assured that God will bless our efforts. We will be following the example of Jesus Christ, who because of His humbleness of mind was ultimately exalted (see Philippians 2:1-11).

TRUST IN GOD

In chapter 2 we saw that sinful pride carries a negative consequence of fear. Selflessness, on the other hand, carries a positive consequence: trust in God. The instant we acknowledge our inability to properly control life, we are forced to appeal to God's power, which is what He planned for us from the beginning. Choosing to openly acknowledge our helplessness creates a willingness to trust.

Several years ago I fractured my leg in two places. The pain was intense—unlike any physical pain I had ever known. I was in a desperate, needy position. Knowing that I lacked the ability to mend my broken leg, I submitted freely to my doctor's orders. When he told me surgery was necessary my response was, "Fine, when do we start?" When he told me about the anesthetic he would use, I said, "You're the doctor; do whatever you must do." When he explained that I must submit to physical therapy afterward, I responded willingly.

Why was I so eager to trust the doctor's guidance? Because I was in a helpless position. My only other choice was to live in misery. I was unwilling to consider such a dreadful option.

In the same way, our prideful decisions to defy God leave us injured. If left unattended, the result can be emotional suicide. Pride leads to fears of rejection, loss of control, and disharmony in relationships. So just as we avert pride by developing a mind-set of selflessness, we remedy our fears by placing complete trust in God. We can declare, "God, since I am helpless to know how to live a proper life, I'll willingly put my trust in you." By placing trust in God we acknowledge that His ways are true. Proverbs 3:5-6 says, "Trust in the Lord with all your heart, and do not lean on your own understanding. In all your ways acknowledge Him, and He will make your paths straight." The following figure illustrates that trust is the answer to our fears.

Figure 3-2

To trust in God means to believe that He is the all-knowing, all-powerful sovereign Being the Bible says He is. And it means being willing to submit to His teachings and directives, even if we do not fully comprehend them. Trust goes beyond mere believing; trust involves doing and being.

A middle-aged woman is experiencing the heartache of an unhappy marriage. Although her husband is not unfaithful, an alcoholic, or a physical abuser, he is an insensitive man who does not choose to act lovingly. This wife fears what she will become if she spends twenty or thirty more years in the relationship. She searches the Scripture for teaching and discovers that she is to show respect to her husband and to have a quiet, gentle spirit. She believes that is impossible. (Actually, she believes that it is not fair that she should set aside her pride in such a manner.) But in honesty she acknowledges that she has not been satisfied any other way. She says, "OK, I'll trust that God knows what He is saying; I'll do it." Even if she does not fully understand this teaching and is not inclined to agree with it, if she chooses to trust she will experience a transformation in herself that will drive out her fears about her future.

The element that makes trust possible is faith. Faith is belief and loyalty not contingent upon tangible proof. Hebrews 11:1 states, "Faith is the assurance of things hoped for, the conviction of things not seen."

My profession pays attention to professional journals. Such journals present experiments that seek to determine what motivates people. They also contain articles attempting to prove theories about such subjects as the proper discipline of children, handling stress effectively, motivating employees by way of positive communications, and how to treat substance abuse. We have theories about many aspects of living. We are trained to examine the data, looking for proofs that tell us which of these theories is valid or invalid.

But the Bible makes no attempt to "prove" that God is who He says He is or that His ways are statistically more sound than mankind's ways. It simply assumes that God knows best. Period. Therefore, the believer who chooses to trust in God may never be able to produce laboratory-perfect experiments to validate His truth. We are instead given the free choice to accept or reject the truth of God based on the revelation He has given us in Jesus Christ.

Those who have reared preschool children can appreciate this principle. Children may not understand our intentions when we tell them to stay out of the street or to go to bed at a certain time. They do not have the capacity to comprehend the world as we do. Parents who love their children say, "Trust me." We know it is futile to conduct experiments to prove our point or to debate our ideas. Instead, we let our child know of the love that is behind the commandments, and we use that love as the basis of trust.

In the same way, God recognizes that humans cannot possibly comprehend all His ways. So He shows us His love and says, "There is no need to fear; trust Me." First John 4:18 says, "There is no fear in love; but perfect love casts out fear." Through Jesus Christ, God has shown us that He has our deepest interests at heart. And as we believe in the depth of His love, we trust, and we experience fewer and fewer fears.

As we determine to place our trust in God, new thoughts guide our emotions and behaviors such as:

- Because I know that it is God's character to be good, righteous, and loving, I choose to trust Him in difficult times.
- God knows what He is doing.
- I'm content in knowing that my life is in the hands of the almighty Creator.
- I can handle things that produce an inward letdown, knowing that He is there to catch me.
- There is no problem so big that it will overwhelm me.

As we learn to place trust in the goodness of God, we do not become unopinionated zombies with no independence of mind. We can still ask questions and seek information. But it does mean that if we come to a point of confusion, we are willing to assume that God's ways are best, even if we are unable to fully grasp them.

FELLOWSHIP

In the last chapter we concluded that loneliness was the third major emotional struggle to result from mankind's fall into sin. A sense of separation was created between mankind and God as well as between fellow humans. We tend to manufacture empty activities (which lead to infatuations, dependencies, and so on) to alleviate our loneliness. Scripture instructs us how to break the grip of loneliness: by accepting God's invitation to fellowship with Him and by sharing that love with fellow humans. First John 1:3, 7 says, "What we have seen and heard we proclaim to you also, that you also may have fellowship with us; and indeed our fellowship is with the Father, and with His Son Jesus Christ. . . . If we walk in the light as He Himself is in the light, we have fellowship with one another." The following figure shows that fellowship is God's answer to our problem of loneliness.

| Loneliness (Gen. 3:9) | → | Fellowship (1 John 1:3, 7) |

Figure 3-3

Fellowship is defined as a companionable relationship. Such a relationship includes sharing deep personal experiences, giving and receiving love, and being united in times of gladness and in times of need. It is God's desire that we know the joy of relationships. Fellowship is what life is all about.

I often ask people to describe their ideas of success. Usually their response is that success means performing the best we can in whatever we do. More theologically minded people often say something about bringing glory to God (still implying good performance). Although I do not negate those ideas, I define success in terms of relationships. Success cannot be attained until deep and satisfying relationships are established, first with God and then with fellow humans. Only when we are clothed in His love can we begin to think about being successful. Although a certain amount of loneliness is inescapable, we can do something to alleviate a large portion of it. For example, Hebrews 10:24-25 teaches us to gather together in assemblies for the purpose of encouraging one another. Ecclesiastes 4:9 instructs us to be joined together with others so we can give aid to each other in times of need. Philippians 2:3-5 instructs us to imitate Christ by developing a sense of humility that looks out for the needs of others. God desires us to become connected to others as a means of fending off loneliness.

Many people dig themselves into deep holes of isolation by living according to prideful desires. The lonely single adult may know that he should reach out to his peers, but he may still say, "I don't feel like making the effort." And although a disgruntled husband may see the need of drawing closer to his wife, he may still say, "This hasn't gotten me anywhere before, so why try?" Such people contribute to their own loneliness.

Lessening the impact of loneliness requires a twofold approach. First, we must accept the fact that because we are all imperfect, loneliness will occur at times. We should not be surprised or threatened by its presence. Second, we must set aside pride and fear to reach out to others in fellowship. As a result loneliness will be minimized.

Louise was a twenty-year-old divorcee who was shy and retiring. When she married out of high school, she was unprepared for the challenges of marriage—as was her husband. She and her husband began experiencing heated arguments. On several occasions he hit her. And at other times he would not come home until the middle of the night. Before their first wedding anniversary they were separated. Divorce papers were finalized a few months later. Louise went home to her parents to hibernate. She spent months seeing no one outside her immediate family.

When Louise came to my office, I could tell that she was eager for something positive to happen. She made plans to continue her education at a nearby college. She decided to get her own apartment in order to reestablish her adult identity. Because her new life-style would have the potential for loneliness, we made plans to confront this issue. First, we examined her attitudes about herself. Although it would never be a joy to experience loneliness, Louise determined that she would not be threatened by it. She made the commitment to renew her trust in God and to fellowship with Him through her prayer life and Bible study time.

As Louise became acclimated to her new routine, she sought out the fellowship of other students. She joined a Christian student's group that met twice a week for meals and Bible study. She found a church that felt comfortable to her. At first she felt uncomfortable around these new associates because none of them had gone through the same harrowing experiences she had. But as she became more open, she learned the contentment of true acceptance by people who know God's love. Louise admits that many times she felt like retreating into her old ways of seclusion and withdrawal. But as she reminded herself of the repercussions of such a choice she determined it was worth the trouble to pursue fellowship. Even though social skills did not come naturally to her, she persisted because she knew that Christian fellowship was the only way out of the pit of loneliness.

Loneliness can be broken when an individual sets aside prideful preoccupations with self, places a deep and abiding trust in the leadership of God, and persists in seeking fellowship both with Him and other like-minded believers. Louise learned that she could not subdue loneliness overnight. But with persistence, she could successfully tame it.

Notice some of the guiding thoughts that can lead a person to choose fellowship over loneliness:

- I was created by God for relationships, so I know He has provided me with the tools necessary to properly engage in wholesome relationships.
- Being open with people is potentially risky, but it is more desirable than closing myself off from others.
- I have a need to seek God through an active habit of prayer and devotion time.
- Other people's needs are important to me.

GOD-GIVEN VALUE

The fourth major emotional struggle to befall sinful mankind is inferiority. Each of us has struggled with some form of insecurity and unworthy feelings. If left unresolved, inferiority can lead to problems in behavior and difficulty in communication.

Scripture teaches that although mankind is responsible for placing himself in a position of inferiority with God, God has chosen to restore him to a position of value. God never intended us to suffer from a sense of unworthiness; that is something we brought upon ourselves by defying Him. The Bible states that He created us "in His image," which indicates that we started life with perfect worth (see Genesis 1:27). And although we have stained our condition, He chooses to return to us that sense of worth. Psalm 8:4-5 says, "What is man that Thou dost take thought of him? And the son of man, that Thou dost care for him? Yet Thou hast made him a little lower than God, and dost crown him with glory and majesty." The following figure illustrates that God-given worth is the scriptural answer to mankind's inferiority.

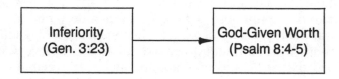

Figure 3-4

We have been crowned by God with glory and majesty! Such an honor has not been given to us as a reward for good behavior, nor is it something that comes and goes at God's whim. This gift of majestic value is offered to us, unmerited, by the God of love, who has chosen to reveal part of His character to us through this unique gift. Even though our sinful ways have caused us to struggle with thoughts and feelings of ineptness, God has responded, "You have defied Me by your sins, but I consider you to be of high worth to Me." We can be lifted from the depths of inferior feelings by accepting God's proclamation as true.

This concept of our God-given value is so elementary that it seems too good to be true. In spite of our error-prone ways, God has made a willful decision to love us as His own children when we enter His eternal family by accepting Christ as the One who died for our sins. So as a consequence, many people feel they have to do something more—anything—to prove their value before God. These people assume they must be emotionally stable, or morally righteous, or spiritually attuned before God will consider them valuable. They humanize God—and consequently detract from His divine nature—by assuming His ways are as mankind's ways.

But when Scripture mentions our worth before God or His care for us, there is no mention of works we must perform. God's pronouncement of human worth is a free gift, and our only task is to accept it. When we accept the gift of His pronouncement of value, we can then think of ideas that are consistent with His offering of love to us and live in ways that demonstrate true appreciation to Him. As we acknowledge our God-given worthiness we will experience a growing inward peace that supersedes the natural predisposition toward inferiority.

Ray experienced transformation in his life when he finally understood his God-given value. He spent forty-one years as a people-pleaser, trying to prove his worth through good deeds. In his childhood he had been a super-performer, excelling in sports and being elected a class officer. His father was a strong driving force who continually pushed him to excel. In his adult years he continued that performance-oriented mentality. He felt that he could demonstrate his value by making lots of money, having an impressive title, and accumulating wealth and fame. Yet in spite of his efforts, Ray felt a nagging insecurity that perpetuated lowly feelings about himself. When he felt a particularly strong urge to bolster his ego, he became involved in sexual affairs. He needed someone to tell him he was OK. His need was actually legitimate. His mistake was to seek the wrong solutions.

In counseling, I asked Ray to tell me his ideas about God, particularly what he assumed God thought about him. Ray said he had always been reluctant to think much about God because he assumed that God was a harsh, forbidding figure. When I said God was indeed holy beyond our comprehension but loving toward sinners, Ray responded, "I wish I could believe that." I encouraged Ray to read the book of John several times, focusing on the love exhibited by the incarnate God, Jesus Christ. When I met with Ray later, he said he was astounded at the patience and kindness Jesus offered to common people. "Is that the way God really is?" he asked. I assured him that although God's perfect holiness caused Him to reject sin, He would accept the sinner into His presence once that person trusted Christ as personal Savior.

Ray made the decision to let Jesus Christ become his Savior, accepting the value and worth that came with it. As a consequence, he was able to put his desire for outward, human confirmations of his worth in perspective and appeal to his value through the sacrifice of Christ.

When an individual acknowledges the validity of his God-given value, new and more meaningful thoughts guide his mind such as:

- There is nothing more powerful and rewarding than to know that God loves me.
- I am OK not because of how great I am but because of how great God is.
- Since I am loved by God, I don't have to depend solely on my human performance for esteem.
- The Lord says there is no such thing as one human who is inferior to another.

KINDHEARTEDNESS

The fifth and final emotional problem resulting from mankind's fall is anger. After Adam and Eve lost the high position of favor with God and perfect communion with each other, they became angry. The need for self-advocacy was born, and, misappropriated, it was easily turned into aggressive anger.

Because there are moments when an antagonistic world produces the need for self-preservation, the Bible cautiously teaches that we will at times have the need to express anger. Ephesians 4:26 tells us to "be angry without sin." James 1:19 tells us to be "slow to anger," and James 1:20 indicates that the anger of sin-prone man is likely to reflect something other than the righteousness of God. So even though we have some instances to "draw the line" in assertive anger, we are taught that there are other, more profitable traits to pursue as a first preference.

Ephesians 4:32 says, "Be kind to one another, tenderhearted, forgiving each other, just as God in Christ also has forgiven you." The following figure shows that kindheartedness should replace anger.

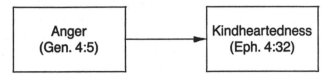

Figure 3-5

Whereas anger is the product of mind dominated by pride, kindheartedness is the product of mind given over to selflessness. Kindheartedness is a deep-seated willingness to give pleasure and to do good. It is characterized by a mild, gentle nature that seeks to put others at ease. Kindheartedness is not something to which we are naturally predisposed, but it can become a regular part of the life submitted to the Holy Spirit.

By stating that kindheartedness is preferred over anger, we imply that we have a choice about our emotional states. The person who recognizes that anger serves no positive function can set aside that emotion in favor of a more appropriate trait. That does not mean the individual represses anger while outwardly feigning pleasure. Rather, the individual deliberately determines to disconnect from that which is creating inner turmoil. The decision to let go of the anger is contingent upon the person's understanding of the greater need the soul has for a kindhearted spirit. This idea is echoed in Proverbs 14:29: "He who is slow to anger has great understanding."

My family history is full of struggles with anger. My grandfather was critical and negative. He directed criticism and harsh speech toward anyone who did not measure up to his strict standards. The screens of his small, wood-framed, two-bedroom house were full of holes because he shot every squirrel that entered his yard. Many times I heard him shout, "Cora, get my gun, there's another squirrel outside!"

Throughout childhood, my father cautioned me about the excesses of anger. He knew that his father's temper had influenced him. Part of his "therapy" was to talk with his children about the need to appeal to God for guidance in kindness and love. I was impressed at his humility. He admitted his need and desired to steer his family toward kindness rather than anger.

As a consequence I have become aware of two things: (1) it is easy for me to feel anger because of my sin nature and my family's history, and (2) as I turn over the control of my life to God, He can subdue my anger and produce kindheartedness. But I must make a conscious decision to allow His kindness into my life. I can never produce it myself. Anger lurks just around the corner waiting for an opportunity to return.

When we make the decision to set aside anger in favor of a kindhearted spirit, we adhere to thoughts such as:

- My life has more purpose as I seek to glorify God with a kind spirit.
- Satisfying the personal needs of others is satisfying to me.
- Rather than standing up for my rights, I will seek to look out for the rights of others.
- Being understanding is the best way to be understood.

THE PROGRESSION OF RESOLUTIONS

Since the five basic emotional struggles are progressive, we can assume that the resolutions to our emotional problems are also progressive. The following figure illustrates how the five solutions presented in this chapter are related.

Kindheartedness cannot be achieved until God-given value, fellowship, trust in God, and selflessness are also realized. Furthermore, none of the traits can be considered complete until the successive traits are attained. For example, selflessness cannot be fully attained until it leads to trust in God, which creates the ability for fellowship, and so on.

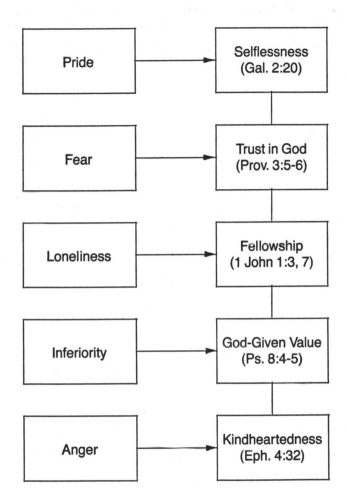

Figure 3-6

We must acknowledge that we will never become perfect in implementing the truths taught in the Scriptures. The Bible teaches that once we come to salvation (justification), we begin the process of growing more and more like Christ (sanctification). However, we will never reach perfection in the process of mental renewal until we are taken into the eternal presence of God (glorification). By acknowledging that, we can head toward mental renewal without becoming disillusioned. As long as we are in our earthen vessels, we must challenge our errant emotions with scripturally based thoughts. Although we will never become perfect in this life, we can press ahead, knowing that God has given us worthy goals.

FOUR
PSYCHOLOGICAL BARRIERS TO EMOTIONAL COMPOSURE

"**I**already know what the Bible says I'm supposed to be doing, so why do I still have so many problems?" I've heard Christians ask that question countless times. It is a good question, and it deserves a good answer.

We have already seen that our emotional and relational problems are a result of sin. Were it not for our decision to defy God, we would not have any of the problems that threaten to undermine the foundations of our lives. Before we can find peace and inner wholeness we must come to terms with our sins and ask God to forgive us and lead us to contented living.

It is too simplistic to say that if we get right with God our lives will fall into order. Don't misunderstand. I genuinely believe that a life crucified in Christ is the only life that is pleasing and acceptable to God and, consequently, the only life that will bring lasting contentment. But I am aware that many Christians have problems that do not go away with increased Bible study and prayer. They need understanding that goes beyond pat answers; they need insight into the factors that make them who they are.

Have you ever been told, "Just pray about it, and your burdens will be lifted," or, "Just give it all to the Lord"? People who offer such advice recognize that dependence on God through Jesus Christ is the answer to each of our personal problems. I have no quarrel with such a thesis. But sometimes other factors must be unraveled and understood before our minds are ready to receive Christ's comfort and direction. Think about how far you would get with the "pray about it" advice in the following illustration.

Jim, a thirty-four-year-old architect, experienced mood swings that ranged between depression and hostile rage. He was twenty-nine when he got married because he had not been able to find anyone who would tolerate his moodiness. He somehow married a wonderful woman whom he believed to be from God. She had a deep spiritual commitment as well as an unusual capacity for patience. Since his marriage, Jim became convicted that his moodiness was a hindrance to his spiritual growth—and potentially to his wife's as well. Also, Jim's wife was pregnant, which sharpened his awareness of his need to develop spiritual leadership. He felt responsible to get his life in order so that he wouldn't drag his new family down with him.

Jim frequently felt unhappy as a growing boy. His father was an alcoholic who ruled through fear and guilt. Jim had repeatedly witnessed his father's verbal and physical rages against his mother. He hated his father's use of intimidation as a means of control, but he was forever puzzled by the fact that his mother seemed incapable of doing anything to rectify the family's problems.

Throughout his childhood Jim attended church regularly. He was taught that the Bible provides all the answers for living, yet he felt that the Bible wasn't pertinent for him. He had a fairly active social life but believed he didn't have much to offer anyone in a friendship. Though he wanted to share love and affection with others, his insecurities with God, his peers, and his family led him to subtly sabotage chances for lasting relationships.

I could see the five basic emotional struggles and their many related feelings in Jim. Not only was Jim suffering from depression and rage, but he clearly had problems with inferiority and guilt, loneliness and despair, fear and defensiveness, and wounded pride. Jim needed to learn to place his trust not in himself but in the Lord's leadership, thereby becoming capable of the fellowship he so rightly desired.

Before we could reach a lasting resolution, we had to clear the hurdles over which Jim had been tripping. If I had told Jim to read his Bible every day, he would have marched out of my office more frustrated than when he came. I wanted to help him use his Christian background in a way that would be pertinent to his needs, but blind spots in his personality needed to be exposed and understood before Jim would be able to appropriate the spiritual teaching he already had.

Keep in mind that the chief goal of examining our emotions is to become aware of our underlying thoughts and beliefs. Before we implement any truth, we must gain a perspective on why we do what we do. The subtle and not so subtle consequences of mankind's fall into sin influence our thought patterns and subsequent emotions. We must be aware of the experiences, past and present, that lead to our personal struggles.

In the last two chapters we have seen that the fall into sin created our basic emotional struggles and their errant underlying mental processes. But Scripture has given us answers to each of our basic emotional problems. In this chapter we will examine four psychological barriers to emotional composure. We can then evaluate our own errant thoughts and beliefs in a new light, replacing them with right thinking.

PSYCHOLOGICAL BARRIERS TO PERSONAL PEACE

DEFICIENT LOVE

In Matthew 22:35-39 Jesus is asked to identify the greatest of the commandments. He answers that the chief aim in life is to love. We are to love God with all our hearts, souls, and minds, and to love others as ourselves. Life becomes satisfying when we know love, and it is incomplete when love is deficient. Because love is the most basic of all needs, we experience emotional struggles when we lack proper love. Personal turmoil can be interpreted as a cry for love.

Developmental psychologists agree on the universal need for love. Infants communicate only at the simplest level, yet they experience the need to be loved. Studies have shown that depriving an infant of consistent love is devastating to his emotional, intellectual, and social development. Without proper experiences of giving and receiving love early in life, it is difficult for us to establish trust and closeness in later relationships.

Most emotional struggles can be traced to inappropriate experiences in giving and receiving love. Rejection by a parent, spouse, or friend ignites such emotional problems as depression, loneliness, guilt, anger, and unworthiness. At the other extreme, smothering love brings an equal number of emotional stresses.

Unsatisfying love experiences fuel the dependent part of the personality. When love is missing in our lives, we lose the ability to handle our emotions in a stable and composed manner. We begin to hunger for love and acceptance (consciously or subconsciously) and become sensitive to a lack in our personal relations. Unsatisfied love can manifest itself in a variety of ways:

- A woman who feels apprehension in her relationship with her father latches onto her husband, unrealistically expecting him to give her a sense of happiness and contentment in life.
- A business man who senses rejection from his coworkers places too much pressure on his family to build him up and make him feel masculine.
- A husband who feels unsatisfied in his love relationship with his wife turns to a mistress.
- A teenager who feels misunderstood by his parents becomes angry, rejecting his parent's values, and follows the crowd.
- A wife who is disillusioned because her husband is not as romantic and tender as she thought he would be sinks into a deep depression.
- A grown woman who has seen her father act unbecomingly toward her mother has difficulty opening up to men.

Those who are deficient in love may find that their behaviors are negatively affected by the actions of others and that their moods fluctuate with the moods of others. They have become too dependent on others for a sense of self-regard. Such dependency is often manifested in anger, unnecessary defensiveness (fear), ultrasensitivity to questions or criticism, and impatience. In addition, the person's ability to give love is usually contingent upon having the stage set by someone else.

Although we all have the need to be loved and to interact with others, I frequently hear people deny that the need exists in them. Such denials usually come from those who are most closed and constricted emotionally. These people often claim that they are not needy and that they don't react negatively to insufficient love. In a sense they deny their need for love to cover the vulnerability and hurts they feel.

It is natural for us to desire human love, but it is dangerous to be too dependent on people for stability in life. Rather, we must acknowledge that our ultimate dependency is not upon humans but upon God Himself. He is our source of sufficiency and contentment. Any time we expect another person to give us the complete feeling of well-being, we run the risk of putting that person in the position of God. We must ask, "Do I believe God loves me deeply enough that I can be composed even when I am not receiving the human love I desire?"

To illustrate how this problem affects our thought processes and our emotions, notice how each of the five basic emotional struggles are influenced by deficient love:

Pride: The individual becomes increasingly preoccupied with self. Feelings of ultra-sensitivity become prominent. Arrogance may emerge as a means of compensation for loss of satisfactory love. Thoughts focus heavily on the rights of self and the desire for prominence and control.

Fear: Fear is common, particularly fear of rejection or fear of failure in personal situations. Thoughts that undermine self-confidence emerge, which result in tension and negative expectations.

Loneliness: A sense of emptiness and meaninglessness emerges. As loneliness increases, it is perpetuated by thoughts of futility and despair. The individual easily imagines others to be uninterested in or detached from him.

Inferiority: The individual has a lowered sense of worth. Thoughts of self-criticism are prominent but so are compensatory thoughts of criticism toward others.

Anger: Anger can be interpreted as a frustrated cry to be loved. The individual struggles with the inner irritation of knowing that life is not as it should be. Thoughts are focused on self-preservation as the angry individual seeks to communicate his desire for more attention and respect.

TRAINED INCOMPETENCE

Think of things in life for which we receive special training. The list is endless. Children are trained to read and write, ride bicycles, add and multiply, draw, and sing. Teenagers are trained to drive, do household chores, write themes, and play sports. Adults are trained to master computers, handle finances, keep up cars, and juggle complicated schedules. Much of the routine of living is boiled down to knowing the how-tos of our particular tasks. But how much training do most of us have in understanding and handling emotions? How many hours of discussion did we have with parents and teachers sorting through our aims and philosophies of communication? How many times did people show love to us and then explain that such love could give us a glimpse of the love God has for us? The answer to these questions is obvious. Most people will have little or no training in the things of life that matter most.

I am convinced that true composure and contentment occur only as individuals comprehend God's plan for the abundant life and live consistently within that plan. But though many people can cite various facts and theories about correct living, knowing God's plan for the abundant life goes far deeper than memorizing ideas. Facts and theories cannot be considered integrated into our lives until they directly influence the thoughts that guide our emotions and behaviors. And before that happens, we must learn to apply scriptural truth to a variety of issues. We must:

- balance self-esteem with humility
- make proper decisions when faced with negative emotions such as worry, anger, or fear
- let God direct positive emotions such as patience and peace
- be principled yet accept others
- be assertive when necessary, silent when necessary
- serve and allow others to serve us
- express love in a way that is satisfying to others and fulfilling to us
- communicate profitably
- respond to inappropriate communication
- develop our spiritual gifts in a manner that glorifies God

Many factors contribute to God's plan for abundant life, and in order to experience it we need specific training. Yet most of us not only received little or no training in how to successfully handle emotional and relational matters, but we were actually trained (ever so subtly) to be incompetent. Consider some of the situations we encounter in the course of a lifetime:

- A schoolboy complains that he is angry with the amount of homework given by his teacher. His mother tells him that being angry will do no good; he should get started on his homework earlier. She doesn't take time to show understanding for his feelings or ask him what he plans to do about his anger.
- A wife expresses bewilderment with the way her two children are constantly bickering. Her husband tells her that she should send them to their rooms for an hour and threaten to ground them if they misbehave again. He doesn't ask

his wife what she thinks her options are or show any particular concern for her emotions.

- A woman expresses frustration to a friend about a problem
  with a coworker. Rather than listening empathetically and
  expressing confidence that she will know how to handle
  herself, the friend tells her that she ought to get out of that
  job and look for a new one.

When we share our problems with others, we tend to receive one thing in return—someone else's answers. Our world
seems obsessed with the assumption that when someone expresses his feelings or burdens, we are supposed to supply a
ready-made solution.

Everything we do communicates our inner beliefs—no
communication is without meaning. And when one individual communicates nothing but unsolicited answers, the underlying message is clear: "I doubt that you have the capacity to
handle your problem correctly, so do yourself a favor and follow my advice." Admittedly, the person may not be sending
such a message intentionally, but once spoken the damage is
done.

Most of us can can recall times when we have been on the
receiving end of such unsolicited advice. Authority figures
provide answers but give little encouragement for making in-
dependent decisions. Well-intentioned parents go to great
lengths to solve their child's problems and deprive the child
of learning how to handle personal struggles. A wife finds that
her husband needs to make all her decisions for her. A husband is stymied by a wife who criticizes but never attempts to
understand. Subtle but powerful messages of incompetence
can hinder us from coming to terms with our feelings and basic beliefs.

Competence must be learned—preferably in the early
years of life. All of us have God-given capabilities that will enable us to balance our emotions. But we are only likely to develop those capabilities if we are encouraged to do so. If we
are not well trained in handling emotions, the five basic emotional struggles will dominate our lives. Notice how they are
affected by emotional incompetence:

Pride: The individual has childish tendencies and views the world from a selfish perspective. Scripture teaches that we each need instruction in setting aside self in favor of God. The person who does not have such instruction remains self-absorbed.

Fear: The individual ill-equipped to work through strained relations and emotional stresses experiences fear. His mind grasps for resolutions to the struggles of life, but solutions are not found. The expression of fear can be obvious (phobias and severe anxiety) or subtle (defensiveness).

Loneliness: Inability to handle emotions creates emptiness. The individual feels set apart. Feelings of helplessness in personal matters cause emotional withdrawal.

Inferiority: No one likes to appear inept. The individual lacking training in emotional issues either collapses in feelings of unworthiness or hides feelings of inferiority by claiming superior knowledge (as in the case of the rigid, all-knowing individual).

Anger: The end product of emotional incompetence is anger. Lacking the ability to handle his own emotions and interactions, the individual lashes out in criticism or becomes passively stubborn. His anger is an attempt to compensate for the frustration of not knowing what to do.

IMPERATIVE THINKING

A man who came to my office for counseling told me that he was an uncompromising man of principles but had experienced years of defeat in virtually all close relationships. People felt their efforts to please him were futile. "Let's put it this way," he said. "My problem is that I'm so right, I'm wrong." I knew exactly what he meant.

Many people suffer from being too right. Through the course of time most of us have developed strong notions regarding the things we believe *should* be included in the good life. For example, we all know that good communication includes both consideration when speaking and proper listening skills. Likewise, we know that hostility and anger do not add to a relationship the way that patience and kindness do. We are full of knowledge regarding correct living.

Although it is good, even necessary, to have well-established ideas about what is right and what is wrong, it is difficult for most of us to maintain composure when circumstances and events go counter to our beliefs. We become impatient and irritable; we experience tightness in our stomachs; we criticize and condemn; we sulk; we feel depressed. It is actually an exception to the rule to have balanced emotions when circumstances go against what we believe. Most of us are at our worst when we feel we are in the right. Note the following examples:

- A wife complains that her husband is not as communicative as he ought to be and is creating a distance in their marriage. As a result she feels deeply depressed.
- A college student knows he has the ability to make good grades, but because of a hectic schedule his grades fall below the standard. The consequence is debilitating guilt that makes him fear his parents.
- A father holds the belief that his children should show him respect. When they don't, he becomes upset and expresses volatile anger.
- A schoolteacher has well-laid plans for her weekly schedule. But upon receiving one setback after another, she declares that she is ready to quit.
- A driver thinks it unfair that others on the highway are so inconsiderate. Becoming impatient with the traffic, he begins darting in and out of the lanes, risking his safety and that of others on the road.

We fall into the trap of emotional turmoil when we don't know what to do with our feelings. Why is that?

Our emotions and communications proceed directly from our thoughts. Beneath the emotions that plague us is usually an *imperative* style of thinking. Imperative thinking defines all issues as right or wrong, proper or improper, and maintains a rigid, duty-bound list of commandments. The imperative individual wishes to reduce events, emotions, and communications into a predictable and controlled agenda. Though he may have a passing realization that the world is mostly gray, the imperative person has the unrealistic desire to see the world in black and white. The imperative individual's beliefs and opinions (however correct they may be) become a burden to his emotional stability.

In order to understand why many of us tend to think imperatively, let's look at how we were taught to behave as children. Most of us received thousands of instructions in our formative years about what we *should* do, what we were not *supposed* to say, how we *ought* to feel, and how we *had* to speak. Before I am misunderstood, I will add that I believe it is healthy to be taught responsible living in formative years. But there is a great difference between being *taught* a needed lesson and having our behavior *dictated* by an authority figure. (In the latter case, the growing child may learn what to do but not necessarily how to reason.) As most of us examine our early years of development, we will recognize that we learned to do what is proper but did not necessarily learn how to handle our emotions and our reactions to uncontrollable events. Many people have learned the rules of right and wrong in such black-and-white terms that they can only cope with their world when it fits the proper mold.

The key emotions that indicate the presence of imperative thought patterns are excessive anger (usually accompanied by criticalness), prolonged depression, false guilt, fear, worry, and impatience. The more prominent these emotions, the more likely imperative thinking is present.

The antithesis to imperative thinking is a more flexible style of thought founded in the concept of freedom. Rather than trying to impose a mental system of obligations upon self and upon others, the composed individual can acknowledge that God has not created us to be puppets or robots designed to simply fulfill obligations. Rather, He created each of us with a free will to decide for ourselves how we respond and interact within ourselves and with the surrounding world. God has no desire that we be controlled by legalistic obligations, and He does not desire us to impose controls on one another. We each have the freedom to determine our level of commitment to Him, which directly affects how we handle our environment. We can choose to live in one of four general ways:

1. We can ignore God and His teachings. Many people do ignore God and experience chaos as a result. But God gives us the freedom to make this choice.
2. We can follow God from a sense of duty, doing the right things not because we want to but because we have to. This choice produces the outward appearance of the good Christian life but an inward propensity toward criticism, irritation, and guilt. The elder brother in the story of the prodigal son lived this way (see Luke 15:11-32).
3. We can fall in and out of God's plan for our lives. We may know some of the basic teachings of God's Word and —when we are in the right mood—follow His lead. But when something comes along that looks better, we stray for a while. This life-style is equivalent to an emotional roller coaster.
4. We can follow God and trust Him, loving Him because He first loved us. With this choice there is no sense of obligation, just gratitude for His mercy and the salvation offered through Jesus Christ. This choice leads to peace.

By offering us freedom, God took a risk. Some will live as He wills; many will not. But apparently that was a risk God was willing to take. In the same vein, we take a risk when we choose freedom over the imperative. When we offer freedom to those around us, there is always the chance that they will treat us irresponsibly. But there is also the possibility that our relationships will take on conviction and commitment.

The same thing is true of our relationship with God. Ideally, accepting His freedom will prompt each of us to ask himself, *Rather than forcing myself to behave in the way I* must *behave, what is my conviction and my choice regarding the way I believe God* wants *me to behave?*

As we give our friends, family members, and coworkers the message "You're free to be who you are," there is a possibility that we will not like the results. But when true freedom is given, acceptance must go with it. And when we offer another genuine acceptance, the risks are actually less, not greater. When we are shown respect and given freedom, we are more likely to respond in love and harmony to those around us.

In my years of counseling, it has become apparent to me that many Christians have taken the teachings of the Bible and used them imperatively for the sake of condemnation. Seeing the Bible as the ultimate list of rules, they impose self-flagellation at the thought of a minor infraction. As a result, they heap upon themselves psychological and emotional problems never intended by God (for example, debilitating guilt, defensiveness, inward anger, inferiority, and so on). Some Christians use their "biblical convictions" as a basis for condemning and criticizing the people nearest to them. They create an atmosphere of tension that undermines the power of God's love.

In attempting to overcome imperative thinking, however, we must not swing over to a life-style of chaos and looseness. Rather, our goal is to develop a style of living that is principled but not condemning, decisive but not coercive, goal-oriented but realistic, and structured without harsh rigidity.

Here is how imperative thinking underlies struggles in the five basic emotional areas:

Pride: Along with imperative thinking comes condescension. The individual who *must* shape his environment into a prescribed mold attempts to assume godlike control over others. Such thinking easily leads to self-absorption and arrogance.

Fear: The individual who fears what might happen to his environment under freedom assumes that people—and even God—cannot be trusted. He must compensate for the shaky status of life by gaining as much control as possible.

Loneliness: A key feature of imperative thinking is that it offers conditional acceptance to others. Because of that, the development of close, sharing relationships is stymied. Isolation and estrangement in relations is common.

Inferiority: On the surface the imperative person may appear to assume a position of superiority. But underlying that front is a powerful sense of insecurity. He actually has a low level of confidence in his ability to handle new situations.

Anger: As imperative thinking continues, anger becomes prominent. The individual has a powerful need to fit life into a mold and is frustrated when things do not fit properly.

MYTHICAL THINKING

In my late adolescent and early adult years I wanted to believe that all human beings were inherently good. As a Christian, I held the idea that God loved the world and was willing to offer redemption to any individual who sought it. I concluded that if God chose to love us on such a grand scale, we must be inherently lovable. I gave only minimal attention to the ugliness of sin and did not even consider the possibility that we could be inherently evil yet loved by God anyway. I realize now that my logic was immature. I chose to indulge a mythical idea.

We are all susceptible to mythical thinking. Mythical thinking happens when we accept a belief system as true without giving it close analysis. For the Christian, mythical thinking has the added dimension of being counter to God's

Word. In a world of stress and strain, we tend to defend ourselves from pain by thinking too idealistically. When the truth hurts, we may fend it off by making up our own version. Sometimes this process is conscious, but more often it occurs on the subconscious or unintentional level. Nevertheless, when we use this unrealistic style of thought, we set ourselves up for emotional struggles. Note some common examples of mythical thinking:

- A husband is upset by his wife's finnicky mannerisms. He does not like the fact that she has always been that way and probably always will be. He thinks that if given enough convincing arguments, she will restructure her disposition.
- A secretary tells a coworker about her boss's inconsiderate nature. They agree that they can't believe anyone could be so rude. They are subconsciously harboring the myth that people should be aware of their personal deficiencies and should therefore get rid of their flaws.
- A girl is insulted by the way a playmate treats her. When she tells her mother about it, Mom proceeds to give her six suggestions about how to remedy the problem. They do not discuss the fact that rifts are inevitable even in the closest of friendships. Subtly the girl learns to think that whenever a relationship problem arises, there will be a perfect solution.
- A minister experiences a prolonged bout with depression. To make matters worse, he feels guilty for feeling depressed. He assumes that if a man in his position were truly close to the Lord, he would never experience such problems. He labels himself a "fake" and resigns his church.

As long as we live, we will be prone to thinking about what might be. Our performance-oriented culture has taught us to believe that if we have a problem, we should be able to latch onto a solution and get rid of whatever creates discomfort. Subtly, we are taught to assume that our problems will cease if we work hard enough. I consider that mentality to be a myth.

Reality compels us to acknowledge that problems will always be with us. And even if we knew the answer to every problem, we would still struggle. If we are truthful with ourselves, we will accept the fact that there is no perfect relationship, no perfect emotional system, and no perfect environment. Although we would be remiss if we made no attempt to change our lives for the better through the power of the Holy Spirit, we must keep a balanced mentality, be aware of the imperfections of the world, and be willing to make allowances for them.

Scripture gives us dual teaching about our humanness and our ability to seek solutions to our problems. Matthew 5:48 tells us to "be perfect" or, more accurately, to aim toward a standard of perfection as we mature. But Romans 3:23 reminds us that we are sinners who will inevitably fall short of the glory of God. We need to balance those two thoughts by seeking God's perfect will while recognizing the impossibility of attaining it in this life.

When we have repeated struggles with worry, anger, guilt, or depression, we are subtly exhibiting surprise at our problems. Such emotions communicate the thought: *I can't believe this has happened.* The family member who harbors resentment toward another implies surprise at that person's behavior. The depressed person's low mood insinuates disbelief in the state of the world. The person burdened with false guilt has bought the notion that self-acceptance requires perfection, and he is shocked each time he falls short.

Jesus said, "You shall know the truth, and the truth shall make you free" (John 8:32). We often think of these words in terms of their theological significance, since they correctly imply that Jesus is the truth and the One who sets us free. But we can also apply them in a broad sense to our emotional selves. As we acknowledge our status as fallen beings in a fallen world, we can reduce our level of shock to our own negative tendencies and to negative circumstances and avoid extremes in our moods. Likewise, as we acknowledge the validity of a life-style devoted to Christ, we will find emotional composure.

Mythical thinking has the following effect on the five basic areas of emotional struggle:

Pride: Our myths have self-serving aspects to them. We choose to believe the things that place our own desires in prominence. That encourages the ego-related emotions of arrogance, hurt feelings, and ultrasensitivity.

Fear: Fears are enhanced by misinformation. If the mind draws from false data, the emotions will follow suit. And there is always the fear that idyllic dreams will not be realized.

Loneliness: Mythical thinking says that we can produce closeness and compatibility in all relationships if we just work hard enough. Failing to accomplish that, we invite increased feelings of loneliness.

Inferiority: The individual who indulges mythical thought will experience a sense of defeat when those ideals are not met. Personal devaluation grows as one's dream world does not materialize.

Anger: The individual's anger is based on shock at circumstances that have not gone according to the ideal. His anger demands a mythical perfection that will never exist.

SUMMARY

Four psychological barriers—deficient love, trained incompetence, imperative thinking, and mythical thinking—hinder our ability to move from emotional turmoil to emotional resolution (see figure 4-1). Our task is to become aware of our emotions and their underlying thought patterns and learn to remove the barriers that block the road to peace.

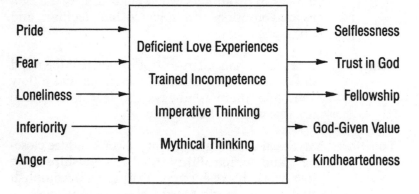

Psychological Barriers

Pride → Deficient Love Experiences → Selflessness

Fear → → Trust in God

Loneliness → Trained Incompetence → Fellowship

Inferiority → Imperative Thinking → God-Given Value

Anger → Mythical Thinking → Kindheartedness

Figure 4-1

FIVE
THE SELF-IMAGE

The book of Ecclesiastes was written by a man trying to make sense out of who he was. In his brief discourse, the author (presumed to be Solomon) uses the word *vanity* approximately forty times. The theme echoed throughout the book is "vanity of vanities, all is vanity." Solomon was faced with situations he considered futile. His resulting anguish came from his discovery that there is no human way to make peace with the world. His image of what the world should be was incompatible with reality. Solomon's problem was that he really did not know who he was.

As ancient as Solomon's problem was, it is a problem that still plagues people today. Civilizations have come and gone, knowledge has increased, and cultural habits have changed, yet human nature remains the same. Even now, in the midst of computerized technology and presumed intellectual enlightenment, anxiety-ridden people are still asking, "Who am I? What am I to think about the way I should live?" Many people live their lives without coming to a satisfactory conclusion. Not knowing the questions to ask or the direction to turn, they exist without a balanced and integrated image of themselves. It is no surprise to discover that these are the very people most prone to emotional and relational struggles. If we experience crises with self-identity, we will surely experience crises in the everyday stresses of living.

Our image of self should be clearly delineated if we are to succeed in making peace with our emotions. What we believe about self directly impacts how we interact with the surrounding world. Since our beliefs and thoughts guide our lives, our core beliefs about self are of utmost influence. With a self-image that is stable and founded on biblical truths, we can properly operate spiritually, emotionally, and relationally. Conversely, as the self-image is distorted, we become thwarted in those same areas of living.

Self-image can be defined as the sum total of an individual's beliefs, thoughts, and impressions about self. It is a mental filtering system through which an individual interacts with his environment. Self-image is not something we are born with; rather, it is learned. Literally thousands of experiences—particularly those in the formative years—are recorded in an individual's subconscious memory bank. Through the years those experiences gradually form the foundation for the guiding thoughts, beliefs, and impressions that determine how we present ourselves to the world.

Experiences that demonstrate one's worth to authority figures, that show competence in completing tasks, and that demonstrate the capacity to reason satisfactorily most directly influence the formation of self-image. One or two events do not shape our view of self. Rather, self-image is forged by the repetition of basic patterns of experience. For example, we all have had traumatic experiences in which we felt rejected by an authority figure. But most of us have had many more positive experiences of genuine acceptance. The few negative experiences will probably not outweigh the positive ones to the extent that our self-image becomes insecure. In addition, each individual has a certain amount of resiliency that causes some of the negative input to be absorbed without completely undermining self-image.

However, some people who have had seemingly healthy backgrounds behave as if they have a weak self-image. Any number of factors, including one's inborn personality type, unusual influences outside one's immediate family, or hidden negative messages in seemingly positive ones, can produce a poor self-image.

Cheryl seemingly had a healthy childhood, but as an adult she displayed the emotions and communications of a person with a troubled self-image. She had repeated problems with a critical, impatient spirit, which caused her to lose many friends as well as the support of her husband and three children. Cheryl said she had a strong self-image, but through counseling she discovered that many of the positive messages she had received from her family had underlying messages that subtly sabotaged her confidence in herself.

For instance, Cheryl had been taught to think highly of herself, even at the expense of others. As a result, her self-image contained prideful ego-boosters that were ultimately destructive. Also, she learned to believe so strongly in her convictions that she reacted emotionally if someone held a different conviction. She was instructed to be careful in performing tasks, but the teaching was so strong that she developed fear and paranoia if anyone responded negatively to her performance. That created an unhealthy need for perfection in both herself and those associated with her. What is more, she had a strong, "take-charge" temperament that caused her to view her world in black-and-white terms. That decreased her ability to be flexible with people and circumstances that did not fit into her mold.

This example illustrates that self-image cannot be discerned by counting the number of positive versus negative statements received. How an individual is taught to sift through the subtleties of human interaction will have a bearing on how an individual learns to view self. The example also illustrates that we can never truly know our self-image until we observe and analyze such factors as outer behaviors, emotional manifestations, and spiritual maturity.

As one who holds the viewpoint of the total depravity of mankind, I believe every human is susceptible to weaknesses in self-image. That is so for two reasons: (1) we are imperfect in our abilities to properly integrate thoughts about who we are, and (2) we are exposed daily to an imperfect world that either intentionally or unintentionally sends messages that are not consistent with God's ideal.

With that in mind, let's examine self-image in a twofold manner. First, we'll explore some of Scripture's direct teachings about who we are. Second, we'll examine some of the tell-tale signs that indicate whether our thoughts about self agree or disagree with those biblical truths.

What We Are

A man complained to me that he was in a constant state of confusion when he tried to understand the Bible. He did not know how to mesh seemingly inconsistent messages such as our inability to flee from sin with the instruction to be perfect as God Himself is perfect. At times God's Word seems to elevate mankind; at other times it offers harsh rebuke. Because the Bible is wholly true, our task is to integrate its teaching into a unified balance.

WE ARE CREATED

The fact that we are created beings may seem obvious. Yet because the secular world constantly promotes its beliefs about evolution, we cannot state that fact strongly enough. In addition, as we contemplate the implications of God's creating mankind, we realize the importance of it to our view of self.

If we were not created by God, we would have license to egocentric behavior. We would assume self-sufficiency in all areas of reasoning, negating the need to look beyond the human mind for guidance. We would assume a position of superiority, viewing God as unnecessary or denying His existence altogether. We would see no need for regeneration, negating any thoughts about sin and the need for a Savior. If we deny our created status, we choose to be governed by sinful pride.

When we acknowledge our createdness, we recognize that we owe our lives to the God of the universe, whose omnipotence and omniscience so supersedes our own character that we are completely dependent on Him. Genesis 2:7 says that man was created out of the dust of the ground. How and why God created man cannot be totally understood. We can only assume that as God spoke the word, human flesh and spirit came into being just as He pleased. His might is so awesome that we must cease our efforts to explain the mechanics of His deeds.

Our accountability to God creates a sense of responsibility that leads to fulfilled living. And most important, by recognizing our created status we gain a deep sense of purpose in life, because each day's activities have significance not merely for the moment but for all eternity. Accepting our created status places devotion to God at the heart of all thought and behavior.

The concept of our createdness has direct implications on behavioral and emotional well-being. If an individual has struggles with interpersonal relationships, he needs to consider how to reconcile his circumstances with God's will.

WE ARE SPECIAL

Genesis 1:27 states that we were created in the image of God. Each person has a dignity that must be acknowledged and respected. Mankind is the only form of creation on earth that has the ability to communicate with God. That truth can serve as the foundation upon which all self-acceptance is built.

Each human being has innate worth and value. Because of His nature, God can create nothing less than the very best. The fact that sin has stained our lives does not detract from our God-given worth. We don't have to do anything to prove our worth to God.

As a minister and psychologist, my father visited many prisons, hospitals, and reformatories. When I was about thirteen, I visited a facility for the mentally retarded with him. As we were given a tour, a young woman resident took a special interest in me. I didn't know what to do. I glanced at my dad. He had a smile on his face and a twinkle in his eye that said, "You're about to make a friend—make the best of it."

The young woman probably weighed two hundred pounds; she had a bowl haircut and an IQ of about 65. She took me by the hand and showed me the things that were important to her. She introduced me as her new boyfriend to anyone who would stop to listen. Although I was a self-conscious and insecure teenager, I eventually loosened up and played along.

When Dad's consultation was over, he pulled me aside and said, "It's easy to love people who look right and act right on the outside. But what you did today was different. You showed love today to someone who may not know much love. And I can promise you, she feels very special right now because of your kindness. And do you know something? The kind of love that you showed to that young woman is exactly the kind of love that God has for us. Whether we deserve it or not, He gives it freely to us. You have learned a valuable lesson today that I hope never leaves you."

To know that we are special in God's eyes enables us to integrate several key ideas into our self-image: (1) we have a base of security to draw from when our human security system fails us; (2) we know that all humans are of equal value, since value is measured not by our deeds but by God; (3) we are born with the capacity to know God, since we have been formed in His image; (4) we know that we were designed to love and to be loved since we bear God's image; and (5) we know that we belong to God.

WE ARE INEPT

To bask in the fact that we are created and special beings would be wonderful. But unfortunately there is more to who we are.

We have already seen that mankind's fall into sin carried emotional repercussions. As a result there are behavioral, relational, and communication problems that we cannot avoid. As hard as we may try, we cannot escape our natural predisposition to sin. In free will we chose to turn our backs upon the life of perfection offered by God. First John 1:8 says, "If we say that we have no sin, we are deceiving ourselves, and the truth is not in us."

When we admit to being sinners, we state that we cannot *not* sin. A day cannot go by without an error in thought or judgment. We do not have the inner ability to be winners on our own efforts. The apostle Paul says in Romans 7:18-19, "For I know that nothing good dwells in me, that is, in my flesh; for the wishing is present in me, but the doing of the good is not. For the good that I wish, I do not do; but I practice the very evil that I do not wish." Paul's frustrations with his sinful inclination represent the frustrations of every individual who intends to do good but fails.

When we choose not to face our ineptness, we drive ourselves into loneliness and anger. We cling to the myth that we would be able to have composure if only the right circumstances were available. We assume that our problems are external. But because we usually cannot change our outer circumstances, we must focus on the things that can be changed inwardly. Lasting transformation can only begin when one's self-image is consistent with Scripture.

It may seem strange to say that positive transformation begins when we admit our ineptness. In the age of positive thinking, this approach seems out of place. But in reality, admitting weakness can be a profitable step toward change. Once we acknowledge our sinfulness, we have a more focused point of attack. We develop a deeper awareness of our real selves and can use it to motivate us to seek help from the ultimate Counselor.

Richard was despondent; his words had a ring of defeat. He told me that he was losing confidence in himself because he failed in a major career challenge. This was the first time he had experienced such failure. Previously he was known in his profession as a success. His competitors would point to him and say, "I wish I had his capabilities." He made friends easily and had power and influence.

Along with his business failure, Richard lost many friends. People questioned his integrity. He felt insecure. And worse, he was uncertain about how to recapture his past status. My response caught him off guard. "This could be the best thing that ever happened to you," I said. Richard began to see that he based his feelings of worth on his own performances. In time he understood that he could still have contentment in his life in spite of his flaws. Though he learned that he was inept, he also learned that the power of Christ could give him the contentment he wanted and needed.

When we admit that we have an inept nature due to our propensity to sin, we lay the groundwork for a belief system that bases self-esteem on a power beyond us.

WE CAN BE STRENGTHENED

The final component of an individual's self-image is the presence of God in his life. But not all people choose to make God a part of their lives. They are incapable of tapping into the strength that He offers, which will ultimately override the ineptness that they are prone to as sinners. But to those who choose to give their lives to Christ, strength is readily available.

On the eve of His arrest and trial, Jesus Christ had a heart-to-heart talk with His disciples. Knowing His words would be His last before His crucifixion, Jesus emphasized basic and important teachings about who He was and how His strength could become the disciples' strength. Jesus said, "I am the vine, you are the branches; he who abides in Me, and I in him, he bears much fruit; for apart from Me you can do nothing" (John 15:5).

Jesus underscored our human frailty ("apart from Me you can do nothing"), but He also taught that we can overcome this frailty if we graft our lives into His. We can claim Him as our God and Redeemer, submitting our minds, our behavior, and our communications to His guidance. Philippians 4:13 says, "I can do all things through Christ who strengthens me." Second Timothy 1:7 says, "But God has not given us a spirit of timidity, but of power and love and discipline." Scripture teaches that we can be strong if we appeal to the might of God offered through Christ.

I can go only so far in my own effort to become patient. For a while I may succeed on my own, but eventually my efforts prove futile, and impatience occurs. I must appeal to God, claiming His patience and letting Him have His way in my activities. Only as I become aware of His presence and guidance can patience occur. And when impatience begins to reappear, I must rethink my position in Christ and reaffirm my commitment to let Him do His work in me. This pattern of focusing on His empowerment must be constant if it is to succeed; otherwise my sin nature returns to the controls.

In essence, the person who becomes strengthened by the power of God deliberately chooses to separate his mind from the sinful enticements that reside within him. He must choose to respond to the immediate presence of Christ in his mind. As this effort is made daily—even hourly—it becomes a pattern, more and more a natural part of the true self.

WHAT WE THINK WE ARE

Because self-image is learned, it varies greatly from person to person. There are three ways to view self-image: too negatively, too positively, or balanced.

THE NEGATIVELY SKEWED MENTALITY

The majority of people who seek counseling view their self-image negatively. These people usually feel inadequate, particularly when handling stressful situations. They commonly indulge in such negative responses as "I can't" and "I don't know." These individuals usually expect negative outcomes to their difficulties.

Frequently people with negative self-images can recite Scripture teaching that God believes we are special and is willing to offer us His strength when we face trials. But when they do recite such Scripture, they inevitably follow it with the word *but*. They may know that there is a better way to think, but they believe it is impossible to make the necessary changes.

For example, a wife who wants to feel more positively about herself may say she can't because her husband is not supportive. A single man who knows that the Bible teaches concepts about claiming contentment may say it is impossible because his dating life is unsatisfactory. A church member who knows about God's forgiveness may cling to his negative self-image because his performances are not up to par. A person can find many reasons to become snared in negative thoughts about self. Why does that occur? There are many reasons, some of which are:

1. *Some people have been given negative messages by significant people.* Tom suffered bouts with insecurity and inferiority. His father, a stern disciplinarian, often told him that he would never amount to anything. When Tom made a mistake or did not complete a chore on time, his dad said that he didn't have any ability. Those negative comments became an integral part of Tom's thinking patterns. In time, Tom did not need to hear his father's negative words; the negative words came to him from his own mind. Self-image will take on the shape of the messages by significant others.

2. *Some people have been taught to feel lowly about themselves.* Sometimes well-intended authority figures, not wanting to promote arrogance or pride, will go too far in emphasizing the ugliness of sin, so much so that the beauty of one's position in Christ is destroyed. The skewed thinking that emerges recognizes only the negative, ignoring or only paying lip-service to God's grace and mercy. One woman said she had a teacher who repeatedly told her class, "You don't want to feel too good about yourself because it will lead to sin." Years later this woman still had those words ringing in her mind. Whenever she was in a particularly good mood, she thought, *Cool it; this will surely lead to sin.* Her early teaching about humility had too strong a grip on her thinking pattern.

3. *Some people cannot determine their worth to significant others.* Many people have not had much negative input from significant others, but they have not had much positive input, either. They may assume negative thoughts about themselves because they lack information that instructs them otherwise. This problem exists in a large percentage of normal families. Family members do not know how to tell each other their feelings, and they are hesitant to sort through sensitive feelings when they do appear. Keeping personal matters hidden and interaction superficial prevents the establishment of a sense of well-being, particularly in the context of solving problems.

4. *Some people are taught that encouragement requires performance.* Too often self-image is closely tied to performance. From early childhood on we learn to think good thoughts about ourselves when we perform well and bad thoughts when we do not. Our standing before humans—rather than God's Word—becomes the foundation for guiding thoughts. Consequently, the individual who has less than perfect performances ascribes to himself negative worth.

THE POSITIVELY SKEWED MENTALITY

Other individuals have developed a too positive view of self. So much focus is placed on the value of self that the concept and consequences of sin are lost. These people either latch onto teachings about their special value to God or declare themselves valuable in and of themselves. But their mental processes are missing the struggles we each have with the flesh. Many times these people couch their views in positive thinking terms that give a nodding wink to God while accentuating mankind's ability to lift himself to greater and greater heights. When this kind of thinking occurs, self-image becomes dangerously linked with humanistic philosophy.

Quite correctly, people who hold the point of view that emphasizes the positive aspects of man proclaim that our thoughts control our behavior. But armed with verses about putting the mind in charge of the personality, they then launch into the notion that if we can just think *enough* positive ideas, we can become what we think. Although this sounds logical at first, it can slowly seduce individuals into false pride. In this skewed mind-set, a subtle arrogance can easily occur. People can become so pleased with what self is that they feel little need for repentance.

Robert came to my office at the request of his wife after she learned that he had been engaged in a long-term affair. Robert exonerated himself of his adultery because he believed he deserved more than his marriage offered him. He explained that his wife seemed too consumed with the chores associated with three school-aged children, so a discreet affair was due him. He told me that he was a Christian, and he explained that God did not want him to be lonely and would understand his dilemma. Robert showed no particular sign of remorse, stating that his major mistake was allowing his wife to find out about his mistress. His guiding thoughts led him to believe that he was special enough to warrant exceptional treatment from God.

Individuals most prone to a positively skewed mentality are those who rationalize the wrongs in their lives with a carefree shrug. Some will admit to having flaws, but will then skirt responsibility by claiming that their problems are "not that serious." Thinking themselves special, they put on mental blinders when faced with the need to reconcile self to sin before God. Their mistake is to select the ego-inflating truths about mankind and ignore or downplay the humbling truths.

THE BALANCED MENTALITY

A healthy self-image strikes a realistic balance between our specialness to God and our propensity toward sin. The balanced self-image is positive, knowing that God chooses to offer unmerited love to all who call upon Him. And knowing that the sinner is capable of creating unspeakable grief in God, there is genuine humility. The positive feeling that comes from experiencing God's love creates unbounded joy in living, whereas the awareness of the ugliness of sin prevents arrogance.

The apostle Paul is a model of the balanced view of self. On one hand he freely acknowledged that his relationship with Christ created contentment (Philippians 4:11). On the other hand he spoke quite humbly, referring to himself as the foremost of sinners (1 Timothy 1:15). Many times he spoke of the glorious feeling he had about life, but in each case he gave all the credit to God rather than to himself.

It was this attitude, then, that led to the development of Paul's bondslave attitude toward Christ. He recognized that the grace and mercy of God freed him from all that was negative about sin, and he committed himself to a lifetime of voluntary servitude to Christ. He accepted his special status before God, and he showed his gratitude by offering God his total will. Although most of us will not attain the consistent submission of the apostle Paul, we can each choose to live our live in subservience to God.

Don struggled for years to become a family and community leader who would please God. As he sought guidance from the Bible and Christian literature, he concluded that God wanted him to strike a balance between firmness of character and gentleness of spirit. Because he understood that God's love and strength could give him a self-confidence that negated the need for defensiveness or timidity, he was able to speak his convictions in a way that encouraged family and friends to take his words seriously. And at the same time, because he knew his weaknesses were the result of his personal fall into sin, he avoided any communication that assumed a false superiority over others. He recognized the superiority of a life-style dominated by the love of God, and he encouraged others to question him about his source of inner strength.

The person who recognizes the sinful ways of self and the love of God for self can live in a way that is both humble and confident. Positive thoughts about self will not restrict service to others.

How We Portray Ourselves

An old adage can help reveal our true perspective on our self-image: Actions speak louder than words. Many individuals are not honest with themselves concerning self-image. I have heard individuals make bold proclamations about a balanced or a confident self-image when, in fact, their behavior did not back up their claims. I have concluded that a person's own opinion is not the most reliable way to determine the nature of his self-image. It is more accurate to examine his attitudes, behaviors, and emotions.

To illustrate how self-image influences us in the five basic areas of emotional struggle and in the psychological barriers to personal growth, notice the contrasts listed in figure 5-1.

Out of Balance	Balanced Self-Image
1. open or subtle pride	1. consistent humility
2. fearful behavior	2. confident trust in God
3. prevalent loneliness	3. natural fellowship
4. feelings of inferiority	4. feelings of equality with others
5. frequent anger	5. frequent kindness
6. too much emotional dependence or independence	6. balanced desire for love
7. poorly handled emotions	7. competently handled emotions
8. imperative black-and-white thinking	8. acceptance of self and others
9. mythical thinking	9. firm grasp of reality

Figure 5-1

RESPONSIBLE VS. IRRESPONSIBLE BEHAVIOR

Our level of willingness to accept responsibility (according to God's guidelines) reveals our inner thoughts about self. The individual who is consistently striving to please God and is considerate of the needs of others probably has a balanced self-image. Likewise, the individual who is inconsistent in accepting responsiblity, choosing to please self instead of God and others, has an unbalanced image of self. He either leans toward a positively skewed self-image that thrives on self-thoughts and places self above God or a negatively skewed self-image that leads to self-depreciating behavior. Examples of irresponsible behaviors that speak of problems in the self-image are: sexual acting out, sloppy job performances, chronic forgetfulness, procrastination, and the quitter's syndrome.

RIGID VS. FLEXIBLE THOUGHT

A flexible mind-set is usually a good indication of an appropriate level of self-confidence. A flexible person is not devoid of opinions. Rather, he holds firm beliefs and ideas while letting others freely hold their own. This person knows that he can be influential in relationships because of his acceptance of others.

On the other hand, the person who is stubborn to the point of becoming critical is insecure about himself. His rigid approach to life requires him to demand complete agreement and compliance from those around him. The rigid person communicates, "I'm not secure enough in my own sense of self-confidence to allow for differences. I require sameness in order to feel OK."

CALMNESS VS. TENSION

Composure is another indicator of appropriate self-image. Individuals who are frequently tense and spend time worrying place undue attention on negatives. *Can't* is a common word in their vocabulary and indicates a lack of belief in their ability to successfully cope with stresses. On the other hand, the genuinely calm person (not to be confused with a passive-aggressive individual) is likely to have deep inner convictions about his God-given value and enabling strength. This calmness is anchored in the knowledge that there is nothing too difficult for God to handle.

BEING REAL VS. BEING SUPERFICIAL

To be real means living life without pretense. What the individual outwardly portrays is consistent with what he inwardly thinks and feels. He does not experience great discrepancy between his public and private world. He does not manipulate or become defensive. Real individuals portray a well-founded sense of comfort about themselves. They accept self, even with its inevitable flaws and imperfections.

On the other hand, some individuals live superficially. Although they have a wide range of feelings and ideas, outwardly they reveal only those aspects of self that presumably keep tensions to a minimum. By living superficially, they illustrate that they are uncomfortable with the full range of self's pluses and minuses. Generally, these individuals have inward feelings of inferiority that indicate a lack of faith in their God-given worth.

BEING RESPECTFUL VS. BEING DISRESPECTFUL

Our interaction with others reveals our attitude about self. What we believe about ourselves naturally spills over into our actions. And the respect that we give ourselves will be consistent with the respect we show others. The individual who believes in the dignity and value of his own nature assumes the same attitude toward others, remembering that "God is not one to show partiality" (NASB*). Consequently, when we show respect and consideration toward others we are illustrating our belief in the worth of God's creation. Likewise, when we demonstrate a lack of respect and consideration for the feelings, needs, and ideas of others, we are communicating our belief that individuals are not important. In turn that reflects on our attitude about ourselves and our status before God. Luke 6:31 says, "And just as you want people to treat you, treat them in the same way."

COMPLAINING VS. ENCOURAGING

The flavor of a person's words are another way of determining his self-image. Does the person focus on what is wrong rather than on what is right? If so, he probably has problems with his self-image. But a tendency to see what is right with one's world usually reflects a healthy and mature self-image. Of course, that does not mean that a balanced individual should ignore problems, choosing to view life with rose-colored glasses. But it does mean that he can turn problem situations into opportunities for growth. By accepting a sense of purpose as a result of our created status and by claiming the strength that is offered by God through Jesus Christ, we can assume that His promise to lead us through trials is true. If we have a solid inner foundation, our words can be encouraging, knowing that we have a God who encourages us. If not, a negative mentality will probably result.

*New American Standard Bible.

REVERENT VS. IRREVERENT

The final test for revealing an individual's self-image is his level of reverence toward God. It is possible for non-Christians to exhibit composure *for a time*. But although some people may be able to illustrate healthy inner thoughts about self by being encouraging, responsible, respectful, or calm, a truly balanced self-image includes a deep, even awe-stricken reverence for God. This reverence goes beyond intellectual acknowledgment of God's existence. To revere God means to wonder at His mercy and might and to express deep and abiding devotion to Him. With reverence comes daily contemplation of God's character and a desire to meditate on His Word and commune with Him in prayer.

Because he has accepted his created status, the balanced person regularly praises his Creator. And because he comprehends his special designation in God's creation, the balanced person consistently communicates his joy to God. Because he acknowledges his sin, the balanced person is reverent and thankful for God's mercy, grace, and forgiveness. And because God offers him the use of His strength in his daily struggles, the balanced person credits God for personal success. Failure to have reverential respect for God shows lack of balance in self-image. Because all that is positive and productive in us comes from Him, we do not have a proper self-image until we reverently acknowledge His work in us.

CONCLUSION

Self-image is made up of our innermost thoughts and ideas about who we are. Yet it is more than that. It is the central belief system from which all other thoughts and actions are derived. It is important then, in the process of personal transformation, to examine this vital aspect of the mind. As the individual shapes his understanding of who he is before God, his self-image will be balanced, and he will demonstrate outward behaviors that reflect his inner beliefs.

SIX
PERSONALITY TYPES AND THEIR DIFFERING NEEDS

Two things can be said with equal certainty: all people are similar, and each individual is unique. Let me clarify that. Romans 5:12 says, "Just as through one man [Adam] sin entered into the world, and death through sin, so death spread to all men, because all sinned." Each of us by virtue of our human imperfection is considered to be "in Adam." That is, every human being is a sinner susceptible to sinful pride. As a result, each of us struggles with the emotions and insecurities that have befallen sinful mankind.

Although Scripture teaches that we are all bonded together as sinners, it also teaches that no two people are exactly alike. The apostle Paul explained the difference among church members by stating, "For the body is not one member, but many" (1 Corinthians 12:14). Paul elaborated by saying that one person may function as a "hand," another as an "ear," and another as an "eye." God has given each person a unique blend of spiritual gifts, strengths and weaknesses, preferences, and mannerisms. Personality traits are so numerous that no one personality will ever be exactly duplicated.

All people have the same nature, but each individual has a unique blend of traits and mannerisms that separate him from the crowd. And although we each need to reconcile ourselves to God through Christ, we all have a different level of fervor (or apathy) to that need based on the way we apply our personalities to spiritual matters.

These two thoughts—all people are similar and each individual is unique—have strong implications for those who seek to understand their emotional selves. That is, although the struggles outlined in the previous chapters are pertinent to every individual, we must also ascertain the aspects of personality that cause one person to differ from another.

Although each personality type needs to examine the major emotional problems discussed in previous chapters, there will be differences in the problems that need focus. In this chapter we will examine the different areas of emphasis required by different personality types. It is impossible to identify each individual with one single label or personality type because we are each unique. Each person will have a mixture of personality types. But for the sake of simplicity, we will examine some common tendencies that distinguish one cluster of individuals from another. We will specify which problems common to that personality type are most likely to hinder his spiritual and psychological transformation.

THE OBSESSIVE-COMPULSIVE PERSONALITY

The obsessive-compulsive personality is distinguished by repetitive, almost unstoppable thought patterns that lead to a powerful need to perform according to a rigid system of duties or obligations. Individuals of this personality type tend to be methodical to the extent of inflexibility. They are uncomfortable with change and variations in routine.

Once obsessive-compulsives get a particular idea in mind, they usually cannot let it go until they have made every effort to act upon it. This creates both a fretting spirit and a finicky nature. These people can become particularly frustrated when they have ideas on which they are unable to act. (For example, an obsessive-compulsive may be unable to relax at home knowing there are assignments left hanging at work.) Obsessive-compulsives are perfectionists who tend to think rigidly. Because of the need to perform "correctly," these individuals are usually impatient with their emotions, because their emotions may interfere with performance. These individuals have an unusual need to appear strong, decisive, and "together," which causes them to experience turmoil in the subjective areas of life—feelings, moments of tenderness, being reflective, and so on.

The two prominent emotional struggles of an obsessive-compulsive are anger and guilt (a spinoff of hidden feelings of inferiority). Anger is frequently displayed by means of strong, habitually critical thoughts. These individuals usually have high levels of frustration with family members, schedules, and the lack of orderliness. They tend to have such a hard-driven need to perform correctly that they become easily distraught when people and circumstances do not suit their desires. They need to explore the various ways they express anger and, more important, the underlying reasons for excessive amounts of that emotion.

Beneath the anger, fueling the intensity of frustration, is usually a powerful struggle with guilt. Depending upon whether the obsessive-compulsive is openly domineering or driven to please others, the guilt can be either subtle or obvious. In the case of the openly domineering obsessive-compulsive, the guilt tends to be obscure. The individual may not openly admit feeling guilty, and may in fact present an aura of superiority. But it is hidden inferiority that propels the drive to achieve. In the case of a more subservient obsessive-compulsive, however, guilt is more readily admitted. This person is usually more open-minded and quicker to reexamine his need to perform for worth that is already God-given.

The psychological barrier most prominent in the obsessive-compulsive is imperative thinking. This personality type is driven by "shoulds," "have tos," and "had betters." Usually this person can point to a long-standing habit, beginning in childhood, of needing to comply with an endless list of rules and regulations. Because the individual may not have felt permission to be free and relaxed, the drive to be a performer was heightened. The obsessive-compulsive should concentrate on reducing imperative thinking and accepting responsible freedom.

THE HISTRIONIC PERSONALITY

Unlike the obsessive-compulsive personality, which is unnaturally driven by logic and the need to perform precisely, the histrionic personality is governed by emotional highs and lows. The subjective dominates this personality. These individuals tend to be more dramatic and excitable, particularly when variations in routine occur. When expressing their feelings (which they do frequently) it is common for these individuals to exaggerate and use superlatives. They tend to have a powerful need for affirmation and attention, which at times produces reactionary behavior (responding before thinking).

Because of their active, emotional nature, histrionic individuals often have charming, gregarious personalities. They have a natural ability to speak about personal matters, and they tend to put most people at ease, particularly in social settings. But this same gregarious, social characteristic is often instrumental in bringing out immature personality traits. Because they need to relate on an emotional, personal level, these individuals tend to be easily upset when the desired level of attention is not received. They may have hidden fears that the "white knight" who will offer them the relational stability and emotional stimulation they desire will never appear.

Perhaps the most prominent emotional struggle for histrionic personalities is loneliness. They may have surface problems with such issues as anger, depression, or worry. But under the surface they have the feeling of being misunderstood and isolated. These individuals, because of an intense desire to be emotionally connected with others, tend to feel that their relationships with family members and friends fall short of their hopes. Consequently, loneliness is germinated and grows into thought patterns that produce anger, depression, and worry.

A second major emotional struggle for the histrionic personality is fear. Typically, the fear of being rejected and abandoned is commonly present (consciously or subconsciously) in these individuals. They are often in a state of apprehension and doubt even when they appear to be happy and full of life. They have an ever-present dread of being disliked or shunned. The psychological barrier most common to the histrionic personality is deficient love. The individual may have a background in which love and acceptance were hard to come by. In many cases, one or both parents lacked the ability to express warmth, leaving that person with a need to look elsewhere for "strokes." Not feeling fulfilled in the area of love, a dependency on others was born.

A second possible scenario involves a family background in which love was given in large doses, to the extent that they were not encouraged to develop emotional independence based on a close walk with God. In this case, they may enter adult life seeking mates and sets of friends who will fill the enormous shoes of the original families. They will most likely meet heartache instead, because mates do not exist who can meet the needs of histrionics in the impossible manner they have come to expect.

THE NARCISSISTIC PERSONALITY

Ancient Greek literature tells the mythical story of a young man named Narcissus, who leaned over the edge of a pond to refresh himself and, upon seeing his own reflection in the water, fell in love with himself. From that story, we derive the term *narcissism*. The narcissistic personality has an excessive, inappropriate admiration for himself to the extent of self-absorption. Narcissists have a difficult time relating to the personal needs of others because of an incessant desire to focus on self. In conversation they have a tendency to repetitively draw the subject of conversation to themselves. For example, when someone is telling a narcissistic person about a personal experience, the narcissist will predictably say, "Oh, that reminds me of a time when I . . ."

This personality type tends to have a long pattern of broken relationships. Although acquaintances may first find them charming and adventuresome, they will eventually discover that these individuals find it impossible to show love and concern. In time, their tendency to be manipulative emerges along with a push for special privileges and considerations. Their level of communication is typically shallow, and their ability to relate to other's feelings proves to be next to nothing.

The prominent emotional struggle in the narcissistic personality is sinful pride. There is an exaggerated feeling of self-importance and a tremendous preoccupation with self's desires and preferences. These individuals have succumbed to Satan's temptation to place self in a godlike position. A positively skewed self-image prompts them to promote their self-worth and ignore their sinfulness and character defects. They need to concentrate on understanding and appropriating biblical selflessness.

Mythical thinking is the psychological barrier most common to narcissists. The delusion of self-importance leads to other delusions. They assume that other people should come to their senses and recognize how wonderful they are. They unrealistically imagine that life would be perfect if only the right person (who worshipfully adored them) could be found. These individuals come from a family background of excessive praise or of the other extreme in which little love was offered, thereby creating a compensatory need for love.

THE BORDERLINE PERSONALITY

The borderline personality is characterized by unpredictable moodiness and inappropriate emotional displays. The term *borderline* stems from the fact that on first impression these individuals seem normal, but on further examination something in their personalities seems incomplete. They differ from the histrionic personality—which is also highly emotional—in that their impulsive behavior and self-destructive actions may include alcohol abuse, sexual promiscuity, binge eating (as in the case of bulimia), and wasteful spending habits. These individuals fear being alone. They feel they must be involved in activities with others and will often compromise their well-taught principles to become connected with others. They need a high level of stimulation and are quickly bored and easily led astray.

In addition to volatile emotional and behavioral patterns, borderline personalities have a high level of uncertainty regarding self-identity. They may have problems feeling satisfied with work or in marriage because they do not know themselves well enough to know what they want. They may make a commitment to one person, life-style, or hobby and, in a matter of months, prefer something else. They may not even know what that something else is, but they know they want something else. The result may be extreme anger and depression, even suicidal depression.

Although these individuals may need to focus initially on the emotional issues of anger and depression, they will need to eventually concentrate on restructuring the self-image. Typically they come from a family background that emphasized superficial qualities such as charming social skills or athletic prowess, or, worse, a background in which love was absent. The result is a foundation of insecurity, which in adult life brings problems with self-identity. As the satisfaction of the individual's preoccupation with self wears thin, he begins a panicky search for another means of stability. That explains the propensity toward promiscuity, craving money, and such.

Borderline personalities often have a background of trained incompetence. Their learning has centered on irrelevant matters, and they have little understanding of such important matters as handling emotions, maintaining personal relationships, and loving without succumbing to sexual arousal. As long as they lack insight into their psychological make-up, they will continue to succumb to their prideful impulses.

THE PASSIVE-AGGRESSIVE PERSONALITY

The passive-aggressive personality is typified by inner frustrations and anxieties that are kept hidden and therefore unresolved. These individuals have an ongoing problem of unresolved anger (which they refer to as frustration or hurt), which causes them a host of problems in interpersonal relationships. They tend to procrastinate, be chronically late for appointments, and be forgetful and lazy. They are often indecisive, not because they have no ability to make sound decisions, but because they would prefer to let someone else take the heat if problems occur. They may seek advice from friends and then ignore it.

In a silent way, passive-aggressive individuals can be controlling. They tend to have a stubborn streak, a critical nature, and a desire to do things according to their own preferences behind the backs of others. In that sense, they may have sneaky ways of being manipulative. It is often difficult to get true commitments from these individuals, and the commitments that are given may prove half-hearted. Hesitant to assume leadership roles, they are often attracted to strong authority figures. Yet eventually their stubbornness creates an unwillingness to be dominated, which sets painful power struggles into motion. They may struggle with marital or family problems, but when confronted with their need to take responsibility in finding solutions they tend to point the finger of blame elsewhere.

The passive-aggressive's most prominent emotional struggle is anger, but the anger is influenced by deep fears. Inwardly, passive-aggressive individuals desire control (sinful pride), but they are afraid that if they are blatant in their maneuvering for control they will be squelched. This fear creates a strong habit of defensiveness and outward phoniness, which over time leads to emptiness in relations. This emptiness eventually turns to anger, but because of the fear of vulnerability, the anger is held inward and is expressed in passive ways. Frequently these individuals become candidates for major depression. Their steps to personal transformation begin with determining how their hidden anger is expressed in an abrasive manner. They need to learn to be more assertive without expressing aggressiveness. In addition, they need to replace fearful defensiveness with trust in God.

In most cases, the prominent psychological barrier to emotional stability for passive-aggressives is imperative thinking. Because of their secret desire for control, they impose a long inner list of "shoulds" and "ought tos" on family and friends. If they can replace imperative thinking with freedom and learn to accept others as they are, they will diminish interpersonal stress.

THE DEPRESSIVE PERSONALITY

People who have longstanding struggles with depression tend to either have passive-aggressive or depressive personalities. The depressive personality differs from the passive-aggressive in that the tendency toward manipulation and defensiveness is not as blatant, nor is there the tendency to get caught in power struggles.

Depressive personalities are distinguished by having long-standing feelings of futility with their own abilities to handle the day-to-day tensions of work or family environments. Feelings of rejection or of just not fitting in play a prominent role in their mental outlook. These individuals suffer from feelings of hopelessness and are often unable to enjoy normally pleasant events. They have lapses of time in which their memory does not serve them well, and there are times when their concentration levels are low. They may think in self-flagellating terms, become easily worried, and feel that life is meaningless. Their motivation to reach out to family and friends is poor. They may have a lowered sex drive and consequently a history of failure or unhappiness in relationships. They may frequently suffer from suicidal thoughts and a desire to die.

Besides the repression of anger, the depressive personality also struggles with inferiority. These individuals have a sinking feeling of unworthiness and despair. They commonly assume that they do not have the same set of tools that enable them to tackle life as productively as others. In many cases they struggle under false guilt from the notion that they are bad. They think in evaluative, comparative terms, and their self-evaluations are unusually harsh.

Most depressive personalities can recall a background in which they lacked satisfying experiences of love. Their parents were either too critical, too uninvolved, or too protective, not allowing them to fend for themselves in the real world. As a result, a negatively skewed self-image was developed. As these individuals developed in late adolescence and early adulthood, they probably had bland social circumstances, preferring to stay with small groups of people, avoiding new or adventuresome environments. In a large percentage of cases, these individuals marry the first or second person they date. Later in adult life they may question the wisdom of that decision.

A major obstacle for the depressive person is the tendency to feel defeated. Since these individuals tend to have a history of disappointment, they do not expect their attempts to change or find a lasting cure to succeed. Their feelings of inadequacy lead to the hope (and even expectation) that other people will accomplish any needed changes for them. They secretly long for someone to wave a magic wand, causing their depression to lift. But as long as those around them continue to "rescue" them from responsibility, they will never make the effort to find their own road to peace.

THE SOCIOPATHIC PERSONALITY

The sociopathic personality is habitually unable to be responsible. These individuals have an impulsive, pleasure-seeking drive that causes them to shun normal moral standards when those standards get in the way of what they want. They frequently experience problems with alcohol abuse, sexual deviancies, or financial difficulties. Although many have higher than average intelligence, they often have a history of poor school or job performances. Living according to hedonistic principles, they seek good times and have a low tolerance for interference of any kind. They are extremely sensitive to any hint of accountability.

Sociopaths do not initially seem to have particular personality deficiencies because they are skilled in creating positive first impressions. And as long as relationships maintain a superficial nature, their selfishness tends not to surface. However, as people try to develop intimacy with sociopathic individuals, they become disillusioned by their propensity toward lying, cheating, and sneaky manipulation. Also, as relationships develop, it becomes evident that these individuals have little depth. (They may be able to speak in seemingly deep thoughts, but that is usually phony). What is worse, when problems in relationships occur, these individuals seem to lack any true sense of guilt, demonstrated by the fact that they are prone to repeating their mistakes. They do not seem to learn from mistakes (except how to be more careful about not getting caught). They seem to have a knack for getting stuck in the same ruts as before.

Although on first impression they may present a friendly, likable disposition, time proves that people of this personality type have an inability to sustain love. They experience the psychological barrier of deficient love. Typically they were either under the care of parents who were extremely strict or extremely loose in discipline. That does not necessarily mean that the parents did not love them, but that these individuals did not perceive satisfactory love. Consequently, they learned early in life that the only way to get anywhere in relationships was to exploit.

Anger is the most prominent emotion in these individuals. It is the driving energy behind their rebellious, free-spirited behavior. Although the anger can be rationalized to be a normal need for self-preservation, it tends to have aggressive overtones, since little consideration is given to how it affects others. It is demonstrated more clearly when sociopathics are required to submit to set structures or strong authorities. When they feel controlled or even hampered or confronted, a nasty temper emerges. Their emotional problems stem from sinful pride and result in an attitude of immunity from normal standards and guidelines. Yet, only by submitting to an accountable structure will these individuals find personal peace.

THE DEPENDENT PERSONALITY

The dependent personality does not necessarily have chronic problems with anger or depression or worry (though that may sometimes be the case). These individuals may, in fact, have a pleasant demeanor and a true servant's heart. If anything, they can be too kind and cooperative. Dependent personalities are characterized by the fact that they have an uncanny knack of finding themselves in relationships where they are in subordination to domineering figures. Their willingness to serve and be kind can actually be exaggerated to the point that they are too tolerant of abusive or unfriendly circumstances. Their willingness to let others take responsibility in major areas of decision-making requires the dependent personality to accept a passive posture as a given in life. An example would be a marital partner who subserviently bows to the demanding nature of his mate, even though the demands are extreme and the mate is obviously taking advantage of the partner's good nature.

The background experience of this personality type tends to be one of trained incompetence. That is, a parent may have specifically taught or just modeled the idea that it does no good to take a firm stand in any issue of controversy, so it would be just as well to smile and do whatever is necessary to keep peace. In learning such a way of thinking, these individuals are specifically denied the encouragement to struggle with options and preferences.

Subtly underlying the dependent personality are struggles with fear and guilt. These individuals like to maintain order in life with little friction. That need can be so great that they become easily threatened by friction, prompting them to do whatever is necessary to keep peace, even if it involves accepting abuse. This habit of trying too hard to keep peace can cause them to take responsibility for the actions of others, sometimes leading them to make excuses for other's flaws or to take blame that is not theirs. This feeds a guilt complex, since they begin feeling badly about themselves whenever someone else strays.

Dependent personalities face problems with troublesome children who have learned to be manipulative, and troublesome marriages in which the spouse has subconsciously accepted the invitation to treat the mate with no respect. In addition to realigning the thoughts guiding them into fear and guilt, they need to learn assertiveness and appropriate expressions of anger as outlined in Ephesians 4:15, 26.

THE CYCLOTHYMIC PERSONALITY

The cyclothymic personality experiences sharp mood swings between elation and depression. Either extreme can last from a couple of days to several weeks. And interspersed between the extremes may even be lulls in which normalcy reigns. When cyclothymic individuals are in the high mood they may appear to be quite enthusiastic, outgoing, pleased with life, and optimistic. They will typically laugh easily and heartily, sometimes even appearing to be giddy. During those times they will attack work with gusto and can be quite productive and creative in thought. There is a danger that in this time of euphoria they may become too impulsive, overextending themselves in emotional commitments, finances, and scheduling.

When the low mood hits, as it predictably does, it comes in part from the knowledge that the high feeling cannot last forever. So the wonderfully happy times come crashing down to disillusionment. During the low moods, cyclothymics can be quite irritable and negative. No amount of encouragement is enough. They question their ability to perform in spite of evidence that speaks well of their abilities. And they view the more effervescent side of their personality as phony. During this low period, they have self-derogatory thoughts accompanied by feelings of loneliness and unhappiness. It is difficult to speak rationally with them at this point, since they are determined to mope and brood.

It is not easy to pinpoint the most specific struggles in this personality type since they can be so varied. In all probability, however, they can be traced to a defensive nature and the inability to accept reality. The family background may have been based on the mythical idea that enough hard work would create ideal circumstances. There was probably an inability, even a fear, of discussing emotions. If emotions were expressed, they were not understood. As a result, the cyclothymic typically refuses to acknowledge problems when things are good and is distraught when things are bad.

These individuals make self-improvement efforts during a depressive period. At that time they are most open to examining their fears and their mythical thinking. As they gain insight into themselves, they need to remind themselves to keep up improvement efforts during times when their moods are positive.

THE SCHIZOID PERSONALITY

The schizoid personality is identified by a chronic inability to develop normal social skills and interpersonal relationships. In fact, these individuals appear to have little ability to express warmth or to engage in the most casual of interactions. They have what is termed "flat affect," or a deficiency in the realm of emotional expression or awareness. When praise is given, they seem unimpressed; when criticism is offered, they appear apathetic. They can be described as plodding through life with dull detachment and passive aloofness. It is no great wonder to discover that they often lack friends or even pleasant acquaintances. If they marry, they tend to be homebodies, but it is not unusual for them to either marry late or not at all.

Usually the schizoid person is motivated toward personal transformation through struggles with depression. However, the depression experienced by schizoid individuals does not always have the same precipitators as the depression experienced by individuals of more normal traits. In most cases of depression the emotion is set up by experiences of rejection, repressed anger, or unusually stressful environmental pressures. But in the case of schizoid individuals, it is usually the by-product of a lifelong history of loneliness and frustration due to an inability in knowing how to relate with others.

Lasting improvement may depend on the availability of a support group who will include these people in their plans. Having someone to show an interest in them will be highly therapeutic. They tend not to be insightful, so making peace with themselves tends to be the by-product of success in relationships. In order to contribute to their own growth process, schizoids need to learn ways of showing appreciation to those with whom they interact.

The psychological barrier most prominent in these individuals is deficient love. That does not mean they necessarily came from a background without love (although that is sometimes the case). Sometimes, there is a problem in their ability to perceive love or to express their thoughts and feelings. That could possibly be due to biochemical problems, to the parents' inability to communicate openly, or to early trauma that inhibited emotional expression. Schizoid personalities will make the greatest therapeutic strides as they experience God's love.

THE PARANOID PERSONALITY

The paranoid personality is characterized by an extremely sensitive emotional state in which the individual's feelings are easily hurt. These individuals tend to be guarded in their words and actions, often suspecting the worst about others. Their defensive nature is prominent and prompts them to fend off criticism or even mild confrontation with denial, rationalization, and blame. Because of the intensity of this defensiveness, they tend to keep their distance in relationships and have a hard time developing closeness. In some cases they are friendly as long as the conversation stays away from anything personal, but they rarely exchange any warmth.

Quite often, anger is the most prominent emotion in their lives. Their need for distance lends itself to a critical nature, usually accompanied by cynicism and skepticism. But although anger is the most publicly displayed emotion, the real issue to be confronted is deep-seated fear. Being sensitive to any hint of appearing weak, paranoid individuals find it difficult to admit to fear. Yet these individuals need to learn to recognize their hypersensitivity as evidence of their fear of being out of control and the fear of rejection. The paranoia is a cover for a weak ego.

Fueling the fear is a stronger than average amount of pride. These individuals tend to be preoccupied with their own importance to the extent that they view themselves as being one of the few normal individuals in an otherwise mixed-up world. This pride causes them to be secretive and controlling, and it pushes them to take positions of leadership so they can call the shots and not be left to submit to anyone else's authority. It is difficult for these individuals to practice submission to God, since they are prone to elevating themselves.

The most prominent psychological barrier for the paranoid person is imperative thinking. Inevitably, these individuals have been reared in backgrounds where life was black and white. Suggestions were not offered nor were opinions truly discussed. Rather, rules were to be abided by regardless of varying opinions.

In befriending the paranoid personality, great care must be taken to establish trust from the beginning of the relationship. Because confrontation is so difficult with these individuals, friends and family members must first demonstrate the ability and willingness to listen to their point of view.

Figure 6-1 summarizes the key elements of each personality type.

CONCLUSION

After attending several seminars detailing the various personality types, a man smiled as he told me: "I had no idea that I was so crazy until I heard the speaker identify the traits of these personalities. I saw myself in almost every one of them!" The truth is, if we took the basic traits of our personalities and examined them in an exaggerated fashion, each of us could place a "neurotic" label on ourselves. Since we are all sinners it is no surprise to uncover weaknesses in ourselves.

But the purpose of explaining these personality types is not to force an uncomfortable title upon someone. Rather, the purpose is to identify the key emotional and behavioral traits that block the process of peace. By facing the most formidable issues, we can begin to restructure our thoughts and behaviors.

Personality Type	Distinguishing Features	Emotional Problems
Obsessive-Compulsive	Rigid system of duties and obligations; repressed emotions; perfectionistic	Anger; guilt; imperative thinking
Histrionic	Highly emotional; outgoing; reactor; personal; need for acceptance	Loneliness; fear; deficient love experience
Narcissistic	Self-centered; impressed by self; broken relationships; shallow; "user"	Pride; positively skewed self-image; mythical thinking
Borderline	Unpredictable moodiness; emotional; self-destructive; Who am I?	Out of balance self-image; trained incompetence; anger
Passive-Aggressive	Repressed anger; indecisive; controlling; critical; manipulative; stubborn	Fear; pride; imperative thinking
Depressive	Rejected; discouraged; hopeless; poor concentration; lowered libido	Inferiority; guilt; anger; deficient love experiences
Sociopathic	Poor morals; superficial; cheating; repetitive mistakes; friendly	Inability for love; anger; pride
Dependent	Dominated; passive; too subservient; pleasant	Emotional incompetence; fear; guilt; need for assertiveness
Cyclothymic	Sharp mood swings; impulsive; easily discouraged; brooding	Defensiveness; poor reality testing; mythical thinking
Schizoid	Flat affect; detached; unimpressed; dull	Loneliness; deficient love experiences; depression
Paranoid	Hypersensitive; defensive; no warmth; cynical	Fear; pride; hidden weak ego

Figure 6-1

Part 2

Yielding Ourselves to God

SEVEN

EXPERIENCING THE PRESENCE OF CHRIST

I have often wondered what it would be like to have a private, face-to-face discussion with Jesus Christ. We would certainly have a lot to talk about. I would be eager to hear Him recount His version of some of the extraordinary experiences of His earthly ministry: the feeding of the five thousand, healing the paralytic man carried to Him by his friends, the encounter with the woman caught in the act of adultery, His trial and crucifixion. I would listen carefully as He would tell about the thoughts and feelings associated with those events. I would try to learn how He determined the course of action to take in each circumstance, and I would try to understand His personality so I could incorporate His character into my own. Surrounded by the peacefulness of His voice, I would feel content.

I am sure that He would be equally eager to hear my thoughts and experiences. He would give me a chance to tell about my burdens and perplexing questions. I would discuss my philosophies, frustrations, and fears and inadequacies with Him, knowing that He possessed the perfect ability to respond to me in a way that would meet my needs specifically. I would ask Him about "gray areas"—how to be humble while resolute, when to be angry and when to set anger aside, or how to know where my will ends and His will begins. His answers would be perfectly balanced. He would be the epitome of the perfect friend. He would know when to question me and when to sit back and listen. He would know when to confront and when to lend support.

As I think about how this imaginary discussion with Jesus Christ would impact my life afterward, I am certain that much more than just His words and philosophies would stand out in my mind. No doubt the greatest impression that would be left by this encounter would be His presence. Although the words He would speak would prompt new thoughts, I would be most drawn to Him not by His words but by His presence. An unforgettable image of a Man who loved as no one else could, One who understood as no one else before, and One who projected a deep and calm confidence and infinite inner peace would be stamped on my mind.

I am anticipating the day when I arrive in heaven and will be able to have such an encounter with Jesus. But at this point in life, I am satisfied in communicating with Him through prayer and the study of His revealed Word. In doing so, I can still grasp the essence of His presence.

Although Jesus ascended to heaven having accomplished in the flesh what He intended, He left behind Spirit-controlled men and women to carry on the task of giving individuals glimpses of His character. Although no individual is able at this time to interact with Jesus in the flesh, born-again believers can be His earthly instruments and can communicate the Person of Jesus Christ to those who are seeking. Through us, others can come to know Him and His message of spiritual wholeness. In His last earthly statement Jesus said to His followers, "You shall receive power when the Holy Spirit has come upon you, and you shall be my witnesses" (Acts 1:8).

This has major implications for the Christian who has come to terms with himself in the Lord. Although we each will have the ultimate desire to feel the personal satisfaction of being loved by Christ, our overriding goal will be to show Christ to those who are still searching. This will be accomplished not just by what we say but by who we are. As we demonstrate the presence of Christ in our own lives, our efforts to find inner peace become complete.

Scott struggled for years with problems of guilt, inferiority, and fear of rejection. His life-style of rebellion and immorality only confounded his problems with the debilitating emotions. In therapy, Scott disclosed many of the reasons for his emotional and behavioral problems. His background had been instrumental in the development of his insecurity and maladaptive ideas. He needed to set aside the guiding thoughts that led to his various personal struggles, choosing instead to focus on the truths of God's Word. In time, Scott experienced a transformation. He became calm and confident a majority of the time, and his behavior was more responsible than before.

Asked by his counselor to recall how he had been able to make such significant changes, Scott said, "As we would share ideas and talk about my emotions, I could see in your eyes that you really cared for me. I knew it was real. And when I would think about the thoughts that God wanted me to have, your concern for me made me know it was OK to accept God's concern as real, too." Scott's reply reflected that the theoretical aspect of counseling had taken a back seat to the experiential aspect.

The counselor's attitude toward Scott was vitally important to his process of making peace with himself. After all, Scott needed a knowledge of God's Word as it applied to the many struggles he had encountered. But the vehicle that carried this knowledge into Scott's heart and mind was the therapeutic relationship. As the counselor was able to project the presence of Jesus, Scott became awakened to the power of His truths. It was when the love of Christ was experienced that the thoughts of Christ were integrated into his mental processes.

In the preceding chapters I discussed two of the prerequisites to finding inner peace: (1) discovering who we are and (2) understanding why we do what we do. At this point we will explore the third ingredient, yielding our lives to God. Specifically, this means that through prayer and concentration we can learn to relate to others in a style consistent with the character of Christ. Since Christ was the model of a life pleasing to God, we will examine several of Christ's traits. By developing these traits, we will deepen our ability to love and minister to those we encounter.

THE TRAITS OF CHRIST IN YOU

RESPECT

An ultimate goal in personal relationships is to show the love of God. We enhance the peace within us by acts of giving, and in the process we can be used as instruments of God.

Ask yourself, *What is the greatest gift I can give to another human?* Although we may be prone to think in terms of material offerings, we must remind ourselves that we are spiritual beings created for relationships. With that in mind, we could conclude that the most meaningful thing we can give another human being is the gift of respect.

Respect can be defined as a caring concern and an unconditional regard for others. The individual who offers respect demonstrates the love of God. And the recipient feels esteemed and valued. The respectful person has no desire to pass judgment, preferring instead to freely allow others to be who they are. It is consistent with the love expressed by Christ: "Come to Me, all who are weary and heavy-laden, and I will give you rest. Take My yoke upon you and learn from Me, for I am gentle and humble in heart" (Matthew 11:28-29).

Offering respect to others is not always natural, even for the mature Christian. Because we are each still in the flesh, we are susceptible to flaws in our abilities to show love.

Several years ago I counseled a man who was repeatedly involved in sexual abuse of children. Although he said that he wanted to change, he was unable to show signs of remorse. He seemed matter-of-fact in his descriptions of his past behaviors. As I listened to this man's misdeeds, I found it difficult to feel respect for him. However, as our sessions continued, I realized that he lacked any experience of real love. His family history was full of violence. I realized that if I would not show positive regard to him, he could spend the rest of his life knowing nothing but emptiness and aggravation. Setting aside my feelings, I let the Holy Spirit use me to communicate that he was valued by God. I began to genuinely care for his spiritual and psychological well being, and it showed on my face and in my tone of voice. I reasoned that if God could love me and desire fellowship with me in spite of my sinfulness, surely I could follow God's lead and exhibit the same toward this hurting man. In time he told me that no one had ever treated him with as much care as I had, and it amazed him because I knew so many negative things about him. My response was to thank God for letting me be used to show His care.

An individual's ability to show consistent respect for others is contingent upon his own relationship with God. Outside the love of God we each have biases and prejudices that create conditional regard for others. Our natural predisposition is to love only those who live within the scope of our own human capacity for acceptance. But those who seek to be Spirit-controlled can determine to set self's prejudices aside, allowing God's unconditional love to be supernaturally communicated. We can learn to operate not on our own ability, but on the ability derived from the indwelling presence of Christ. We can echo Paul's statement in Galatians 2:20: "It is not I who live, but Christ who lives in me."

It is impossible to overestimate others' need for Christian love and respect. Because we were each created by God for relational love, it is the deepest need that can be known. And because our sinful world is flawed in its ability to give love, respect is a gift not given with sufficient frequency. As we learn to show respect to those who come into our lives, we communicate, "I truly want God's best for you. You are valued and significant." As this is done, we demonstrate that we are at peace with ourselves and that we want others to experience peace too.

EMPATHY

John 11:35 is the shortest verse in the Bible: "Jesus wept." Some people had approached Jesus with the news that His close friend Lazarus was dying. When they asked Jesus to hurry to Lazarus's side, He did not rush, knowing that God was going to work a miracle. By the time Jesus neared Lazarus's home in Bethany, Lazarus had been dead four days. Outside the village, Jesus greeted Lazarus's sister Martha, who then summoned her sister Mary. As Mary approached Jesus, she broke into tears, expressing tremendous anguish. As her emotions flowed, Jesus is said to have been deeply moved in spirit, becoming troubled. It was then that Jesus joined Mary in her tears. Jesus did not cry because He felt helpless in the circumstances; He had already predicted that He would miraculously heal Lazarus. Rather, His outpouring of emotions occurred because He had empathized with Mary, and He felt her hurt and her brokenness as if it were His own. He was so involved in her communication that He had completely absorbed the essence of her spirit.

Empathy creates a bond between people and builds a spirit of cohesiveness enabling them to attend to each other's words and feelings. Empathy can be defined as a vicarious experiencing of the thoughts, emotions, and perceptions of another individual that creates a powerful understanding of that person's perspective. It includes an awareness and a sensitivity to that individual's unique inner struggles.

In order for empathy to be a significant factor in relationships, it is not enough that it be felt; it must also be clearly communicated. That is, it is not enough for an empathizer to merely understand the other person's unique perspective; the understanding must be clearly communicated before empathy is complete. This communication can be transmitted verbally in a reflective statement such as, "When people ignore you, a deep hurt develops, and it must cause you to feel very disillusioned." Or perhaps the empathy can be communicated with a caring, knowing facial expression or nod of the head. As empathy is communicated, the recipient feels attached to one who is capable of comprehending his struggles, and consequently he becomes a trusted friend whose suggestions, opinions, and reflections are taken seriously.

The process of establishing empathy can begin literally in the first minute of contact. As an individual shares personal feelings or experiences, the empathizer can make it his task to feel and communicate something of that person's uniqueness in relation to the subjects expressed. Clarifying questions can be asked, such as, "How did it feel to know that your supervisor cited you as being the one employee he could always count on?" Identifying statements may be offered: "As I put myself in your shoes, I can only imagine how bewildering it must feel to be so alone." Restatement of the individual's words can be given: "So when your husband speaks rudely, all you know to do is to sit tight and keep your mouth closed." Throughout the interaction process, these and other statements can be consistently expressed as a means of letting the individual know that his point of view is understood.

Concentration is vital in establishing this trait. The empathizer must be someone who has resolved that his own sinful pride will not get in the way of understanding the other person. That is, the empathizer does not want to have an "agenda" that creates impatience and the desire to control. Nor does the empathizer need to be preoccupied with other matters such as mentally planning the day's schedule, worrying about making the "right" response, or making judgments about that person's character. The overwhelming desire to feel *with* the individual in his expressions and experiences is the major factor that causes empathy to be genuinely transmitted.

The necessity of empathy in our lives underscores again the fact that we were created by God for relationships, and we cannot experience true inner peace until we give of ourselves in understanding others. The need in those around us is so universal that the one who does not empathize is missing a basic element of living. In early childhood development, emotional attachment must first be established before a child can integrate intellectual stimulation. And in the adult years, this sequence is still necessary. Consequently, one's effort to find peace is not likely to be successful until the ability to place self into the shoes of others is consistently practiced.

WARMTH

Almost every person can dredge up memories of a school-teacher whose disposition was as sour as the day was long. That teacher may have made it a point to teach her lessons thoroughly, but her lack of warmth negated the possibility that what was learned would be enthusiastically recalled after her days of giving examinations were completed.

Warmth is a necessary trait. We may be intelligent in a wide range of subjects, but if we are detached, the relationship will never get off the ground. Warmth communicated in the spoken word, tone of voice, and facial expression is an adjunct to the traits of respect and empathy. A warm demeanor reveals the characteristics inside a person that might otherwise go unnoticed.

In Mark 10:13-16 young children are brought to Jesus so that He might touch them. Christ must have been enamored by the children's innocence. Yet while this was happening His disciples rebuked the people and told them to leave Jesus alone. Jesus responded, "Permit the children to come to Me; do not hinder them." As much as anything else, I'm sure Jesus was hurt to think that He would be deprived of the chance to share Himself with little ones who absorbed His warmth like sponges. In fact, this passage reiterates that He then took the children in His arms and blessed them.

Imagine the gentleness exuding from Christ as He was swarmed by His young admirers. No doubt the parents went away that day having learned a prime lesson in the art of loving. They had seen how the Man of peace was naturally at ease with children. His character was filled with a warmth that attracted the most sensitive and intuitive of people. Jesus' warm demeanor was a vehicle that carried His love to the heart of the recipient.

Warmth can be defined as a comfortable feeling of well-being and compassion conducive to the establishment of friendship and relational security. As warmth is expressed, personal relationships that convey closeness and caring develop. The recipient senses that it is acceptable to expose his deepest thoughts and feelings, knowing the atmosphere offers acceptance and gentleness.

Some individuals desperately need a caring interchange from someone who has mastered Christian warmth. One woman came to my office on the heels of a divorce proclaiming that she hated all men. Both her father and her husband were abusive. I realized this woman needed to be treated tenderly.

Although I was interested in her thoughts, I also knew that she could not change her ideas without some experience to validate what I wanted her to learn. After a few individual sessions I encouraged her to join in group therapy, knowing it would offer her a more natural experience of warm interchanges than individual counseling. When she was ready to terminate counseling, she specifically recalled her early statement about hating all men. With a sigh of relief she stated that she had new hope because of her experiences with compassionate men.

When people seek to establish relationships, it is possible that they may feel weak, overwhelmed, or highly frustrated. Consequently they need a relationship with an individual who does not add to the stress. When warmth is present, anxiety is reduced, and eventually one begins to feel confident in the relationship, knowing that it offers safety and comfort. Because the experience of God's presence is essential to relational growth, it can be accomplished when an atmosphere consistent with His care is fostered.

SUBMISSION TO GOD

Since inner peace is derived from the belief that God's Word offers the ultimate truth to our emotional struggles, an integral part of maintaining that peace is to practice genuine submission to God. This means foremost that the believer knows about God not merely in an intellectual manner but through a personal experience. He will declare publicly that he has voluntarily decided to set aside self's preferences for sin with a commitment to allow Jesus Christ to be Savior and Master. This specifically implies that when the believer relates to others, there will be an understanding that he has a deep allegiance to the will of God. Others will notice that a special ingredient is present in his life.

What was the most excruciating emotional experience in Jesus' life? Some might choose His trial or His agony on the cross. But while those events certainly created anguish, I would choose Jesus' time of prayer in the Garden of Gethsemane immediately prior to His arrest. It was then that He was praying so fervently that sweat like drops of blood poured from Him. He even asked His Father that if He would will it, the impending task might be removed from Him. But He also said, "Yet not my will, but Thine be done." It was this attitude that carried Him through the mock trial and the humiliation of being made sin on the cross in our behalf.

Submission to the authority of the Father was a cornerstone element in the peace that Jesus Christ experienced while in the flesh. If questioned or ridiculed by crowds, He maintained composure knowing that His inner stability came from being connected with the Father. If faced by Satan and his temptations, His submissiveness carried Him through. When weary because of His disciples' lack of faith, He stayed patiently by them because of His awareness of His mission for the Father. In all that He did, a submissive spirit permeated His being, which then influenced His manner of interacting with others. He was at peace with Himself because He knew His position before the Father.

Each day in my counseling office I am faced with individuals who have the knowledge of God's Word but lack inner peace because the element of submission to God is missing. Many of these people have professed belief in Christ as Savior, but it is a belief of their intellect, not of their entire being. Consequently, anxiety, anger, impatience, and the like are regular ingredients in the personality. There has not been a complete letting go of the controls of one's emotions. Subservience to God occurs only when convenient.

I am struck by the reaction of many people (Christian and non-Christian) to the word *submission.* It arouses contempt from people who believe submissiveness cheats them of their personhood. Many women feel belittled when a speaker suggests that a submissive spirit is a vital ingredient in healthy family relations or in church organizations. They assume that this insinuates that they will become nonentities. Many men bristle when it is suggested that they too should develop a heart of a servant, setting self aside and acquiescing to an Authority higher than themselves.

Yet if I correctly understand the character of Christ, submission to God does not relegate women to a doormat position, nor does it make mice out of men. On the contrary, as we submit to God we attain a greater status. By submitting to God we attain an identity and purpose that is by far superior to anything this world can offer.

Thomas sought counseling for periods of depression. Thomas performed well in his profession, and when his performances were at their peak he felt happy and content. But when he hit a snare that led to struggle and failure, the depression would appear. For years his emotions were like a swinging pendulum, alternating between feelings of success and defeat. I challenged Thomas to evaluate the commitment that he had made to God ten years earlier. Although Thomas had publicly professed Christ as Savior and had grown in the knowledge of Scripture, he did not feel that his life was truly a mission for God. As we discussed what full submission to God implied, Thomas acknowledged his need to reconstruct his ideas about success. He realized that lasting success—and its subsequent feeling of contentment—comes not through performing perfectly but through living in daily awareness that he is a representative of God whose purpose is to show the world God's love.

Many individuals seek an affair or a divorce because they have lost their love for their mates. Knowing this is not what God wants them to do, they do it anyway, and inevitably they reap the emotional consequences. Individuals with homosexual leanings go against God's natural laws and succumb to a life-style of sin. Drug and alcohol abusers pollute their bodies with unnatural substances. Other individuals engage in poor communication practices that are recognizably in contradiction to biblical principles.

When we submit to God's guidance, we not only are recognizing His supreme authority and holiness, but we are laying claim to the benefits and natural consequences of an alignment with that which is truly good. So rather than being something that detracts from a person's identity, submission to God adds to our quality of life.

OBJECTIVITY

A person at peace with self is characterized by objectivity. Objectivity can be defined as being uninfluenced by emotion or prejudice to the extent that another person's revelation does not adversely affect the ability to relate with logic and fairness. In contrast, the individual who lacks objectivity is easily disturbed or offended, which creates an inability to get beyond the superficial aspects of an individual's communications, succumbing instead to one's own biases and frailties. Whereas the nonobjective person becomes ensnared by another's struggles, the objective individual is able to empathize with others' emotions and experiences without the loss of personal composure and reasoning.

Not too long ago a man was dragged into my counseling office by his wife, who had caught him in an adulterous relationship. The man obviously did not want to be there, and within minutes he was pointing his finger at me, telling me that I was *not* going to make him succumb to my Christian beliefs. After a five-minute tirade, during which time he used profanity and derogatory language, I calmly told him that I was glad to know how he felt about counseling since such knowledge would assist me in communicating with him. Fully expecting me to be just as angry as he was, this man was confused by my response. Although the man wanted to fight with me, I remained understanding and unoffended. That objectivity gave him an illustration of a rational style of communicating. Several sessions later he thanked me for being patient rather than offended toward his emotional explosion.

Before a single conversation occurs between ourselves and others, we must remind ourselves that every person alive is or has been afflicted with a wide variety of stresses and strains. No one is immune due to the fact that we each live in a depraved world. Consequently, before an emotional outburst occurs or an unflattering experience is shared, the objective listener will do well to brace for the unexpected. All humans are capable of untold sins, and we must recognize that no individual is going to live without some difficulty with matters of sin. Even the individuals who outwardly appear to be fine Christians can have significant struggles with the flesh. Knowing and accepting the truth about who we are as sinners can keep us from being shocked by exposures to an individual's sins.

A classic example of personal objectivity is Jesus' encounter with the woman at the well in John 4. The fact that the woman was at the well during midday indicated that she had experienced interpersonal problems—otherwise she would have drawn water early in the morning with the rest of the women. In her initial conversation with Jesus she was curt, but her mood soon turned to curiosity as Jesus spoke about living water. When Jesus mentioned her husband she was defensive, and when He revealed that He was aware of her five previous marriages as well as her current adulterous relationship, she was awestruck. Throughout the conversation the woman was confused about what she should think. But Jesus maintained His objectivity because He had resolved to be unshaken by her personal struggles. In His mind He had ideas about how best to speak with this woman, and He proceeded according to those well-conceived thoughts rather than reacting to her emotional instability.

In the same way the person at peace with self can maintain personal composure by having a sound knowledge that "all have sinned and fall short of God's glory." Knowing this, a balance can be struck between emotional involvement with others and intellectual detachment.

The applications of this trait are numerous. Think, for example, of the fewer arguments married couples would have if they learned to objectively understand the strengths and weaknesses of one another without feeling the need to react to the inevitable flaws. Or imagine how a parent could maintain a more consistent composure if he recognized that his children will make mistakes by virtue of the fact that they are mere mortals who cannot be expected to handle all circumstances with perfection and maturity. Or picture the difference in work settings or church and social gatherings if we each would rationally acknowledge that differences are a part of groups, and that mistakes are bound to occur. The emotional calm that is a part of gaining personal awareness and understanding could be maintained for rewarding lengths of time.

CONFIDENCE

Jesus was not an insecure person; in fact, He had tremendous confidence in Himself. He was not prone to cowering when someone would attempt to corner Him with loaded questions. On the contrary, when He spoke, He exuded authority and certainty in a manner that astounded crowds (see Matthew 7:28-29). Knowing who He was and what He was about, Jesus Christ was able to maintain a consistency of inner confidence. The person who has made peace with himself can have this trait, too.

The level of personal confidence is extremely important to the life-style of a composed individual. This confidence can be three-directional: toward God, toward self, and toward others. More defined, that means that (1) God has revealed all the necessary standards for proper living in a way that can be clearly understood by each person; (2) as we appeal to the power and direction of God, God will supply us with the ability to do His will; and (3) others can have wholeness in their lives as they are introduced to the strength that comes from knowing Him.

The confidence of a contented individual can be defined as faith and assurance in one's personal abilities based on the knowledge that the Holy Spirit will guide one's efforts with discernment. It is this confidence that enables an individual to project himself as one who can be trusted and believed. By definition, this confidence does not include arrogance or a desire for dominance. Instead, it assumes a lack of fear or embarrassment and the presence of composure and certainty.

Perhaps one of the greatest repercussions of an individual's confidence is the hope it can instill in those near us. Family, friends, and acquaintances often look for someone to give signals that say, "When difficulties arise, we can handle them." They are looking for a person who offers hope. And when hope is present, those people's minds can be awakened to optimism and expectancy for the prospect of successful relationships. Without it, we can feel pessimistic and unmotivated to make the effort required in relationships. The confidence exuded by the person at peace with himself can subtly but powerfully transmit the message that God's strength is present, and it can thereby create an atmosphere conducive to healthy relationships.

I vividly recall hearing a public testimony given by a man, James, who had once been caught in the throes of depression for several months. In his testimony James told how he had experienced lifelong problems of insecurity and passivity. Not feeling competent to take a stand for his most basic needs and desires, he had stumbled through an unstable career and through an unsteady marriage. He readily admitted that his childhood had not prepared him for the rigors of adult life, and as each year had passed he became more prone to depression. Feeling hopeless, James sought professional Christian counseling. He stated his apprehension about opening himself to a complete stranger. "I felt like I was disrobing myself in broad daylight, leaving myself psychologically naked to this man. I'd never done anything like it before." As the session unfolded the counselor had outlined some of the key issues in this man's life that could profitably be explored. James's eyes lit up as he said, "After I told the counselor my story and he shared his initial impressions, he looked straight at me and said, 'You know, if we both are committed to the work to be done here, you can change.' Imagine that! He told me I could change. Nobody had ever said that to me before. I was absolutely elated!"

More than astounding theories and insights, James had been looking for a reason to hope. And he found it the moment the counselor had expressed a confidence in their ability to make things happen. Literally, this single factor had been the key that spawned a readiness in him to challenge his thinking patterns. The counselor had become a significant model for James, and his belief in God's ability to work in them became the springboard for a successful series of sessions which taught him a new way of life. By means of a calm, assured manner the message had been communicated: "There is no problem so overwhelming that it will totally defeat you. With the help of God, things don't have to be the way they are." James's illustration shows that the counselor's sense of confidence was not merely a self-contained trait. It was contagious.

GENUINENESS

So far we have discussed how several characteristics can be present when a person has come to have the presence of Christ within. But each of the traits discussed will have an empty ring if it is not also accompanied by genuineness. Although this trait is intangible, its presence can be readily discerned by those who are observing our behaviors for cues to signal that we can be trusted. Whether we like it or not, other people may be skeptical when we act respectful or empathetic or confident. So consciously or subconsciously they will be looking for verifications that speak of the genuineness of our actions.

Genuineness is defined as being worthy of belief. The genuine individual lives without pretense, free from the burden of facades and unnecessary performances. A composure is present that communicates, "I am at peace with myself, and I have contentment." No particular effort is made to "sell" oneself because the genuine person is willing to let others formulate their opinions as they will. Consequently, others sense that when words are spoken they are sincere; when care is expressed it is from the heart.

Several years ago I spoke with a minister who made the decision to leave the pastorate to pursue a career in construction. He told me that his heart had never been committed to "professional ministry." For several years as he had struggled with the many demands placed on him. He had to force patience. He was frequently discouraged when people did not grow spiritually at the rate he wished. Often his mind would wander as someone would recount a personal experience, and he was not certain if the encouragement he offered was of much help. He explained, "I felt like I was acting in a role that should have been filled by someone other than me." He had rightly concluded that he was not a good candidate for a pastor. Although he was a fine Christian who knew much about the Bible, he did not have that extra measure of genuineness enabling him to pastor in a believable way.

Genuineness presupposes several factors: first and foremost, one's Christian life-style must be more of a desire than a duty. To be genuinely credible, the individual must have the deep conviction in his heart that God's love is a specific preference placed on his heart by God Himself. Such things as kindness and patience are not practiced because of Christian obligation but because of a fervor to live in such a manner. Second, the genuine individual is one who has thought about his beliefs on a broad range of subjects and is capable of expressing convictions and preferences that are not merely theoretical or borrowed, but they are one's own. Third, there is a well-integrated conception about the profoundness of knowing God's holiness and living with an awareness of it. The individual understands that we are spiritual beings first and the ability to lovingly relate to another is accomplished as one becomes attuned to his own position before God. Fourth, the individual is aware of his own tremendous ability to sin, resulting in real humility that causes him to sidestep the temptation to be superior, choosing to speak with others rather than to them. Fifth, the individual is not controlled by fear and defensiveness, but is open to feedback and is willing to make himself vulnerable. In doing so, he sets an example worthy of following and becomes a friend to the those in need. Then finally, there is a willingness to communicate immediate feelings and reactions in an unrehearsed manner, modeling healthy communication for others.

Most people we encounter have been exposed to relationships that are anything but genuine. They have known the fear of having to be guarded in the expression of hurt feelings or controversial thoughts, and they have been exposed to hundreds of circumstances requiring "proper" performances. They have felt rejection when flaws have been revealed to friends or family members, consequently creating a hesitancy in the acceptance of themselves and of others. It is predictable that most people will welcome a relationship that not only allows realness but encourages it. We can become a living illustration of wholeness that can inspire others toward openness and authenticity in relationships.

There are times when tactful self-disclosures can augment the atmosphere of genuineness. Rather than presenting oneself as a stodgy individual who is beyond problems, it can be helpful to tactfully expose our own humanness. I specifically recall the shock in one woman's face when I told her I could identify with her feelings of futility when her children were disobedient. When I told her we had similar moments in our household she quickly retorted, "I know you don't have any problems at your house; you just can't." Chuckling, I told her that our goal can be to handle our struggles as they appear rather than hoping they will go away forever. By my simple self-disclosure I let her know that I could personally identify with her emotions while also having a well-conceived plan to face them.

In summary, finding peace with oneself cannot be considered complete until there is also an ability to respond to others in a manner that illustrates the presence of God's guiding hand. As we share His love with those nearest us, we experience the satisfaction of knowing that we are consistent with His character.

EIGHT
COMMUNICATION SKILLS
AND TECHNIQUES

All of us have been in the awkward circumstance of not
knowing what to say or do. Think for a moment about
your first date. Do you remember how you fidgeted for the
right words at the front door? And can you recall the self-con-
sciousness you felt when your manners proved to be barbaric
at best? It's humbling just to think about it, isn't it?

I wish I could promise that awkward communication
would be nonexistent once we reach adulthood. But you already know better than that. We have no guarantee at the beginning of each day that each interpersonal exchange will
proceed without a hitch. The majority of us simply have not
been trained to communicate smoothly in every circumstance. And even those of us who have received training in
communication skills will sheepishly admit that we frequently stray from our textbook knowledge. Simply stated, relating
to others does not come automatically and effortlessly. It
takes discipline!

Up to this point, we have made an effort to understand
ourselves both psychologically and spiritually in an effort to
find the road to peace. It is invaluable to know how sin influences human nature and how the Scripture teaches us to
overcome our struggles. And it is therapeutic to understand
how our family background has influenced our patterns of
emotions. But we can't stop there if we desire to come full cir-
cle to a life of contentment. We each have a need to structure
our communications in such a way that our interchanges can

be fully rewarding. This is particularly true as it relates to our ability to communicate with the people closest to us.

COMMUNICATING SKILLS AND TECHNIQUES

In relating to those closest to us, we are called upon to communicate in ways that illustrate and enhance emotional composure. Consequently, it would be helpful to contemplate the skills and techniques that are an intricate part of knowing how to relate more effectively and deeply with others. As we learn to incorporate loving communication into our lifestyles, we continue in the effort to yield ourselves to God's guidance. In conjunction with the traits listed in chapter 7 (respect, empathy, warmth, and so on), these communication tools can help us express God's love to those around us.

We will look at eight skills that can change the course of our lives if we will let them.

ATTENDING

We must begin by learning to *attend* to the thoughts, feelings, and perceptions of others. Attending can be defined as directing careful concentration toward someone. It is expressed through eye contact, alertness, facial expressions, and appropriate reactions. It provides tangible evidence of our genuine care for another. When we attend to another's words, feelings, and expressions, we create an atmosphere conducive to sharing God's grace. The person we are with begins to think: "I am being taken seriously, and as a result I will be all the more committed to building up this relationship." The significance this takes can be phenomenal.

I can still recall a very early experience in my clinical internship that taught me the value of attending. A woman had come to our clinic distraught because her husband had abandoned her and her infant son. She was full of emotion and desperately seeking someone who could understand her plight. When I asked her to tell me her experiences, she poured out her soul with tears and anguish. For most of the session, I let her talk and I expressed concern and understanding for her feelings. My voice was soft and my heart was sincere. She went into a long discourse about the trials of her marriage. It was clear that she was in need of a good listening ear. As our session came to a close, however, I had an unsettled feeling because we had not taken the time to discuss in depth some ideas that I thought would help her in her emotional struggles. As she stood up to leave she told me that it had literally been years since anyone had taken the time to show so much concern for her. She had been so starved for attention that the very fact that I showed interest was therapeutic. My attentiveness proved far more valuable than I had realized.

Everything we do communicates something. No act is devoid of significance. We may assume that relationships succeed when we share pleasant events with or know significant facts about someone. But true bonding does not occur until the other person receives clear and consistent communication that says: "You're important to me." This is done with good eye contact, a knowing nod, inquisitive remarks, a pleasant demeanor, and a show of appropriate concern. By noticing the subtle and obvious cues of friends, we set the stage for genuine communication. The other person begins to feel that there is a purpose in relating, and he gains affirmation of his self-worth.

It must be emphasized that attending is not merely a ploy that can be easily faked. Nor is it a skill that can be taught from a textbook. In order to communicate genuine interest, we must have genuine, God-given compassion for the needs of those around us. Anything short of that would eventually be exposed as insincere.

By attending to the expressions and needs of others, we can learn to overcome our preoccupation with self and the pride that leads us into sin. If we practice attending, we practice humility and follow Christ's example of giving esteem to others.

SOLICITING

Most of us have fantasized about relationships that are open and honest. Yet in reality we find that much of our communication is structured and phony. Most of us won't let down our public veneers without some prodding. I recall conferring with a woman who was curious to know if I had made any headway at all in private discussions with her husband. Although I have ethical guidelines that restricted me from sharing our conversations, I did tell her that we experienced some true soul searching interchanges. Shocked, she told me that she rarely heard him say anything of a personal nature, so she was eager to know how I had pulled any self-revelations from him. "Simple," I told her. "I asked him."

Kicking around theoretical ideas or facts and figures is not the same thing as communicating. In close relationships, we want to structure our communication in ways that encourage personal interchange. That is part of what makes relationships successful. If we discuss ideas without revealing what lies inside us, our communication becomes impersonal. Our discussions become more profitable when we know the uniqueness of the other person. But because some individuals are hesitant to boldly blurt out their deepest thoughts or because they may not know which self-disclosures are going to be accepted, we may need to solicit the things that will enhance the personal dimension of a relationship.

Soliciting is defined as a method of questioning that encourages another to openly share feelings, experiences, and ideas in a way that leads us to better know that person. It enables the solicitor to more fully understand the meaning inherent in that person's behaviors, emotions, and communications. Soliciting brings personal enlightenment, because it creates an atmosphere that aids the process of self-discovery. Although soliciting involves asking questions, it is much more than that. It can also include expressions of interest in matters close to another's heart, of confusion regarding vague subjects, or of encouragement to continue with communication that is incomplete. Let's keep in mind that soliciting is entirely different from being snoopy, since its goal is to create greater intimacy rather than to acquire juicy tidbits for gossip or manipulation.

I must admit that when I don my counselor's hat, soliciting is a far easier task than it is when I am in an environment where less heavy subjects are explored. You see, many counselees would be surprised, even perhaps disappointed, if I did not seek to ascertain disclosures that supersede normal relationships. But this is not necessarily the case in more normal settings. Even so, I believe that many, if not most, individuals would be willing to let themselves be more deeply known if a genuine, nonthreatening opportunity were presented to them.

We must be careful not to use solicitation as a predetermined program or simply a means to an end. Instead we should see it as a way to communicate genuine interest in the other person and to build confidence in the relationship. When we communicate openly, our relationships gain depth. We will find greater rewards by risking vulnerablity than by hiding behind masks of phoniness.

The extent of our soliciting will vary depending on whether we are among family members, friends, or casual acquaintances. But the mechanics are the same. Whether you are speaking as a wife to a husband at the dinner table or a church member to a visitor, you can show an interest in the person by soliciting their thoughts and feelings. Without being pushy or presumptive, you gently create an atmosphere that says, "I'm interested in you."

ACTIVE LISTENING

After we have solicited information from someone, it is important that we listen to his feelings, thoughts, and experiences. The role of active listening in communication cannot be overstated. Without this element, relationships cannot be expected to mature. Each individual has a unique combination of feelings, thoughts, and perceptions, and the listener needs not only to hear the words spoken but to gain a perspective of the other person's uniqueness. That can be done only by taking time for contemplation.

Active listening is not the same as sitting quietly while waiting for a turn to speak. Rather, it is hearing and contemplating the messages sent by the speaker. It requires concentration to get into the other person's frame of reference. It is so vital to the outcome of successful relationships that it can be considered essential if personal interactions are to meet their objectives.

Active listening is distiguished from mere hearing when the individual communicates that he or she is listening. For example, if an acquaintance tells you about the sadness she feels as a close friend moves away, you can respond by paraphrasing what you believe to be her feelings: "It leaves you feeling empty, doesn't it?" If someone suffering from an unwanted divorce says in anger: "It makes me so mad that our family is being disrupted by this nonsense!" you might empathetically add: "I can tell; it's really eating away at you." The speaker then has the knowledge of being heard, and a loving bond is formed in the relationship. Such bonding becomes an important step toward trust and acceptance in the growing relationship.

You will notice that as you actively listen, you can gain insight into the things that are most pertinent to the speaker —his innermost feelings and struggles as well as his hopes and joys. It leads to empathy—understanding the world from the other person's unique perspective. To that end, you feel you truly *know* the individual in the deepest sense.

Success in relationships does not occur merely as a result of exchanging interesting information. Because we are each social creatures, we each have the inborn need to be affirmed and understood. The mind may hold facts about many individuals, but if I do not interact with their feelings, the information can be labeled as trivia that does little to enhance our relationship. Listening encourages us to develop Christian compassion in every relationship.

CLARIFICATION

All interpersonal communication is subect to confusion and frustration. After all, we are each unique and will approach events in varying ways. This should not cause alarm; it is just a fact. Consequently, it is not unusual for us to misunderstand those around us. When we are confused by what someone has said, we need to request clarification. Clarification can be defined as communication that is intended to ease confusion. When clarification is employed properly, vague statements are made more specific, contradictory expressions and feelings are brought into focus and examined, words are applied to feelings that had eluded definition, specific statements replace broad generalities, and examples illustrate key feelings. All of this is done in the interest of bringing ideas, perceptions, and feelings into clear focus.

As an example, there are many times when the clarifier will ask the speaker to explain in more detail the meaning of an expression used. Perhaps a friend who tells of a tense emotional system can be asked to elucidate what happens during these "uptight" times, due to the fact that this expression can mean so many different things. Or a single man who speaks of disillusionment with women may be asked to explain what he means when he says he is disillusioned, particularly if the listener feels this is a term that is being used to veil deeper feelings of anger. Perhaps a marital partner will state that she and her husband do not communicate well, so the clarifier might ask for an example of a time in which the communication breaks down. In each of these cases, the intent is to draw the problem discussed into clearer focus, which then enables all parties involved to be more certain of the direction they will take in talking with each other.

After several counseling sessions, one woman told me that she had learned to be much more specific in the way she spoke with herself. She told me: "You have asked me so many times to clarify what I mean that now I do it automatically to myself. It's getting to the point that I won't let myself get away with making vague complaints that just keep me feeling depressed." She had learned the value of being specific in the way she spoke with herself. She realized that when she spoke in broad generalities or in clichéd terms, she only kept her problems alive.

As we learn to encourage clarity of expression in our homes and friendships, we can keep minor problems from developing into major ones. As an example, have you ever misinterpreted a friend's silence to mean rejection when in fact the person was merely weary? A clarifying question at such a time could keep anxiety low, preventing an erroneous, perhaps painful, reaction. As we gain proficiency in clarification, we will bring peace to our lives.

SILENCE

There are times when the best thing to say to a friend or family member is nothing at all. Keeping in mind that communication occurs even without the exchange of words, the perceptive communicator recognizes that at times a spoken word can actually detract from the mood of the moment. By knowing when to be silent, we exhibit sensitivity to another's needs. By speaking too quickly or too frequently, we betray our need to maintain control or our feelings of discomfort during silences.

Examples of times when silence is required may include the following:

• The individual is steeped in thought trying to find the right words to express a delicate matter.
• A very deep and painful emotion is expressed and a response would detract from the mood of the moment.
• Tears are being shed, and there is a need to let them run their course.
• The individual is struggling to recollect an important memory from the past that has always been rather blurred.
• The individual is hesitant and is trying to determine how to "break the ice" in a conversation.

By being silent when necessary, we offer the other person greater freedom of expression in that he is allowed to determine his own course of self-expression. In addition, we are showing patience with him and his feelings. Once we learn to adjust to them, silences can set a mood of comfort and provide a soothing lull in the flow of conversation.

The therapeutic impact of silence was brought home to me in a very powerful way when I was counseling a young man named Philip who had been previously misdiagnosed by another doctor as paranoid schizophrenic. Indeed, he was slow of speech, which made him appear sluggish of mind. But it was clear to me that he had more "on the ball" than he had previously been given credit for. In one session, he told me that he felt the need to share with me some very delicate experiences of rejection by a close coworker. He started by saying that he was ashamed of himself for the things that had happened in this relationship. Then he hesitated and stared down at the floor for what seemed to be a long pause (probably about two minutes). During this pause I sensed that it would be inappropriate for me to pick up the conversation and move it on to something livelier so we just sat quietly. Finally, I broke the silence by asking very softly: "Would you like to share your thoughts with me?" He told me that he had paused because he was trying to decide if he should tell me a delicate piece of information. He then explained: "Somehow I get the feeling that I can trust you, so I'm going to tell you everything." He then proceeded to tell me that he felt guilty because he had indulged homosexual thoughts toward the rejecting coworker. Although he had never acted in a homosexual manner, he was very afraid to reveal himself to anyone for fear of what that person might think. (I began to understand why the other doctor had assumed the erroneous diagnosis.) I was firmly convinced as he talked with me that if I had pushed him for information during his moment of silent struggle, Philip would not have opened his soul to me as he did. My silence made him feel that he was not being rushed, nor was he working with a "pushy" counselor. Consequently, he had been able to determine within himself that it was safe to disclose such a delicate problem to me.

During the course of any heart-to-heart interchange, some thought-provoking ideas may be discussed. So it is quite possible, even desirable, that we will want to take some moments of reflection to become aware of reactions and impressions toward the matters under consideration. Silence offers the availability for this to occur. Meted out in balanced doses, it allows for the process of reflection and self-examination to take root in a significant way.

CONFRONTATION

I assume that the person at peace with self has the desire to become intricately involved in others' lives. It is not sufficient for a person to develop self-understanding for the purpose of mere intellectual exercise. And one of the ways to become personally engaged with others is to properly confront them when necessary. Loving confrontation creates a closeness in a way passive acceptance cannot. And because of personality differences and flaws in character, it is a necessary ingredient in healthy relationships. In fact, in Ephesians 4:15, believers are encouraged to speak the truth in love with one another as they grow together in Christ.

Loving confrontation is defined as constructively exposing and examining behavior with the intent of bringing unresolved conflicts into focus. It enables the recipient to incorporate information about self that can help him become more specifically attuned to the needs vital to personal growth. Confrontation is part of the give and take of relationships in that it prompts the individual to consider the impressions and perceptions that his or her behaviors leave with others. It differs from common criticism in that it lacks the aura of judgment, and it does not have any ulterior motives related to coercion.

Successful confrontation requires that the confronter offer acceptance and objectivity and that the recipient recognize it. When confrontation is made in a judicious manner, great care is given to discern the person's readiness. Before you confront, think carefully about whether the confrontation will be beneficial over the course of time.

Confrontation may be direct or gentle. In the case of someone who has been brazenly sidestepping crucial subjects of discussion, you might say, "You're avoiding the real subject again. Let's get back on track." But in the case of someone's avoiding a sensitive topic due to timidity or guilt, you might begin, "I've noticed something about the way you have responded to this subject. Would you like to hear it?" The keys to productive confrontation are sensitivity and tact. Sensitivity comes as we practice the skill of attending.

The key elements that signal the need for confrontation are (1) improper behaviors or (2) denial. In view of this, confrontation is considered to be a major tool intended to create honest examination of feelings and needs. To illustrate, I recall one woman who sought counseling because her seven-year-old daughter was suffering from recurrent stomach disorders. Her family doctor directed her to counseling to determine what might be corrected in the family style of communication. (This woman was also on the brink of losing her husband due to his feeling of being dominated and browbeaten.) In the first few sessions we discussed key issues such as her imperative style of communication and her subtle use of passive-aggressive anger. We noted how she had been taught such habits in her own dictatorial family background.

As our sessions unfolded it became increasingly apparent to me that this woman was politely tolerating my observations with no real intentions of making any alterations in her guiding thoughts. Knowing that I needed to "add some spice" to our therapy before she decided it was all an exercise in futility, I confronted her by saying: "I'd like to make an observation. I've been discussing with you some distinctly pertinent issues that are part of the reason for the tension in your life. I detect that you are humoring me, but because it is not particularly what you want to hear, you are letting our discussions stay in this office. It doesn't appear you are giving serious thoughts to them away from here. Because of the very delicate and possibly explosive nature of your circumstances, I would strongly encourage you to carefully consider your motives for seeking counseling. If it seems that we are just spinning our wheels, perhaps we should reconsider the advisability of continued sessions."

At first this woman was taken by surprise. No one had spoken quite so directly to her in a long time. She told me she would think about what I was saying, but truthfully I did not know if she would come back. But sure enough, the next week she returned and told me that my confrontation had made a big impact on her. She began to rethink in earnest the things we had discussed and had concluded that indeed she needed to strongly consider the insights we had talked about.

Obviously, there are risks inherent in confrontation. The confronter can be misconstrued as being unempathetic or controlling. Also, because timing is such a delicate matter, it could come at a time when the recipient is not ready to respond to it. Consequently, a prerequisite to confrontation is the development of a genuinely caring relationship and a keen understanding of the needs and idiosyncrasies of the individual. It is clear that there were times when Jesus Christ chose to confront individuals, but it must always be understood that He first developed a reputation as a compassionate, aware individual.

In our personal lives, family relations require the most sensitivity in confrontation. Because of daily exposure to one another's differences and quirks, it is easy to take the relationship for granted in such a way that directive communication is offered with little or no compassion. Consequently, it must be stressed that confrontation should not occur until the one confronting is certain that he has already built a reputation for acceptance, and that the confrontation is not inconsistent with a message of love.

SELF-DISCLOSURE

Our ultimate goal in any relationship is to know and be known. That is only accomplished when we are willing to expose ourselves to others. In so doing, we become models who encourage authenticity. In a world that promotes phoniness and pretense, it is significant when we learn to openly acknowledge ourselves to another. In doing so, we tend to live more honestly before God as well.

Often, we are prevented from confident self-revelation by two distinct obstacles. First, we may feel that self-disclosure is too risky. Second, we are inexperienced in appropriate ways of sharing ourselves with someone else. When these obstacles exist, we look to others for indications that self-disclosure is safe.

Personal self-disclosure is defined as divulging parts of the deeper, inner self with the intent of exhibiting realness toward those with whom we relate. It does not include the need to "air dirty laundry" before others, but it is a means of letting someone know that we experience the same basic emotions and psychological barriers that they do. It should not be practiced to the extent that it creates an impression of self-preoccupation. It is done to prevent us from remaining a mysterious, unknown entity to others.

As an illustration, I must admit how easily I can identify with the individual who is very performance oriented, to the extent that an overabundance of mental and physical energy is given to life's varied pursuits. Being a doer and an achiever, I can identify with the need for significance and the fear of failure that so frequently thrusts individuals into struggles with impatience or imperative thinking or guilt motivation. Consequently, when I talk with people of like mentality, I will at times share my ability to understand such struggles due to my own past experiences. Without going into excessive detail, I will let these individuals know that I have experienced the tension and impatience that is part of the "performance package." Then if I ever advise that person to live within a mentality of freedom, willfully choosing kindness over impatience, it is known that I am speaking as one who "has been there." This tactic is much like the style of relating used by the apostle Paul, who would occasionally interject autobiographical information as he witnessed publicly or wrote words of instruction to fellow believers.

One man in particular comes to mind who illustrates the impact of realness in the development of a relationship. After three or four discussions with each other, this man told me: "Before I got to know you, I told myself that I would walk away immediately if you came at me with a bunch of 'Christian theories.' But you seem to speak with me from the heart, and I know that you know what I'm talking about." Keeping my own personal windows open to him made him feel that he could trust me with his innermost needs and feelings. Others feel more capable of acting in a more genuine manner when we willfully (and in proper amounts) become a model for true genuineness. Relationships become less of a plastic exchange of facts and data, and more of an attempt to allow authenticity to take root.

INTERPRETATION

Because two people can hear the same sentence and perceive two entirely different meanings, there are times when interpretation is needed. Interpretation is defined as discerning the meaning of behavior to the extent that the true significance of that behavior is understandable. Interpretation goes beyond the technique of clarification in that it seeks to discern the definition and significance of external matters. By interpreting, communicators learn to "read between the lines," picking up hidden subtleties in interactions. It is through interpretation that the "meaty" aspects of relating occur.

In order to successfully interpret, it is necessary that the interpreter listen to more than just the words being spoken. Rather, it is necessary to listen for the implicit messages behind the facade of normal communication. The interpreter seeks to put words and significance to inner thoughts that the speaker may not be overtly stating. As an example, consider the case of a woman, Emily, who had many regular mood swings ranging from euphoria to depression, from love to hate. It became obvious that her extremes in mood were very closely tied to the love and affirmation given or not given by others. Trying to get at the heart of the matter, I said to her: "On the surface, I hear that you have many changing moods that come and go with the ways people treat you. But beneath the surface, I hear a very lonely person crying out for love. You must have a more-powerful-than-average need to be loved." As soon as I said this, Emily confirmed with tears that I had hit the nail on the head. So rather than speaking immediately to the more superficial aspects of her life, we launched into an interchange regarding her longstanding feelings of loneliness. By interpreting the meaning of her mood swings, our communications developed depth and Emily felt that she was in the presence of someone truly interested in her real self.

When seeking to make interpretations of behaviors, there are two avenues available. First, the interpreter can state directly: "Here's what I am sensing." This can be a legitimate style of interpretation when the person is unaccustomed to overtly stating his true feelings. The second style of interpretation is to lead the person to read the meaning of his behaviors by asking probing questions. Ultimately, this technique can prove highly profitable since it encourages the individual to think reflectively. It also creates mental strength in that person because the interpreter eventually enables others to become more capable in self-confrontation.

When friends and family members make interpretive statements to each other, their relationships become fuller. There is a lack of pretense and a presence of authenticity. Satisfaction grows because they feel connected with each other.

Unfortunately, we tend to feel inhibited when using this communication technique with our friends and family. After all, think of how paranoid we could become if we thought each of our words and actions was going to be subject to immediate interpretation. Yet close examination of our personal encounters reveals that interpretation can be extremely helpful in creating in-depth interactions. For example, suppose a husband notices that his wife is in a melancholy mood, moping as she goes about her daily routine. Rather than restating the obvious, he might say, "I suspect you're still disappointed about the argument you had with your mother last night. It must make you feel defeated in your efforts to be kind to her." Going beyond the facts to her feelings, the husband shows a willingness to be involved with his wife in a deep, meaningful way. In this sense, interpretation is not so much an analytical tool as a device that draws another person closer.

NINE
THE PROCESS OF FINDING EMOTIONAL PEACE

So far, we have developed a broad understanding of some key issues that contribute to our guiding thoughts and ideas. We are now ready to piece together our discussion and examine how the full process of making peace with oneself unfolds.

As you plan to implement the insights we have discussed, remember to focus on the deeper meanings of emotions and perceptions rather than getting bogged down with surface matters. Many people wrongly prefer to concentrate merely on behaviorial matters without recognizing a deeper need to understand the thinking patterns, the emotions, and the background deficiencies that are at the root of the problems.

Discovering what lies at the heart of the personality is not an easy task. However, there are steps we may take to come to terms with our troublesome emotions. Let's look at the five major aspects of growth essential for completing the process of finding emotional peace.

FIVE STEPS TO MAKING PEACE WITH OUR EMOTIONS

1. Identify the various inner struggles and recognize how and when they manifest themselves.
2. Understand how past experiences influence your current struggles.
3. Identify the guiding thoughts and ideas that are at the base of your personal struggles.

4. Recognize how your struggles feed on each other.
5. Develop a growth strategy that converts inward changes to outward changes in your behavior and communication.

Step 1: Identify your inner struggles and recognize how and when they manifest themselves.

Appraise your background deficiencies. This is not as easy as it may appear. Most people are not trained in clearly identifying and labeling their personality features. We tend to establish in our minds well entrenched defensive systems (such as rationalization, denial, and repression) that keep us from accurately identifying our emotional struggles and thinking patterns. So, as a first step in renewing the mind, we need to make a very clear and honest appraisal of our emotional struggles and background deficiencies.

Consider a construction superintendent who has a very powerful style of communication with people. He may not be aware of the levels of inward turmoil that are underlying his "high and mighty" style of interaction. As he examines some of the inner tensions that feed his behavior, he may likely acknowledge certain frustrations. Those can be the beginning points for the process of mental renewal.

Or consider a pessimistically minded woman who holds anger inward, not really admitting to herself the breadth of her emotion. Underlying her pessimistic thoughts are the feelings that influence her communication style. She needs to learn that anger is not always exhibited outwardly or aggressively. It can be evidenced by a sour disposition, by sarcastic retorts, or by cold stares. When she learns to recognize how this emotion is portrayed in her daily life, she will begin to develop a balanced self-image that will influence her expressions.

Examine the circumstances. After we recognize our emotional struggles, we need to identify the circumstances in which these struggles most commonly surface.

For example, a husband has just returned home after a difficult day at the office where he was dragged through a set of problems. At this point he is most vulnerable to having his anger drawn out by an insensitive remark or action by his wife.

We need to be aware of the times, the people, and the circumstances that are likely to trigger our defense systems. A knowledge of those mechanisms will help us better focus on what triggers our anger and also to concentrate on developing the thoughts and steps we need to take to control it.

Focus on how you resolve your emotional problems. This can be an eye-opening experience. For many it is the first time they gain an awareness of the underlying causes of their lifestyle. Unresolved emotions, errant thinking patterns, and deficiencies in love experiences are often the discoveries of this process.

For example, a person who has identified guilt as a primary emotional problem may discover that it not only manifests itself when he is being reprimanded by an authority figure, but that it can also dominate his mind when favors are asked of him, when his spouse makes a mistake, or when he pursues leisurely activities. The more we know of how and in what circumstances our emotions are displayed, the more capable we will be to restructure our mental processes.

Clearly, this tactic of identifying our problems and recognizing how and when they surface in various circumstances will be utilized over and over throughout the course of self-discovery. Because of the complexity of our problems, the potential always exists for finding new insights or new twists to old insights. The person who believes he "has arrived" at a level of full understanding of himself needs to expand his awareness of the complexities of his human personality. As long as we are on this side of heaven, we have sin to contend with and will never be at a loss for personal problems to identify.

Identifying the most pressing issues that are creating problems is an invaluable part of the self-discovery process. We need to eliminate the blind spots that will prevent us from discovering our true personal make-up. As inner struggles are clearly understood, the objective part of the mind gains a distinct advantage over the subjective.

Step 2: Understand how past experiences influence your current struggles.

The past is too pertinent to be brushed aside. Because we are creatures of habit, it is relevant for us to comprehend how our current habits (in handling emotions and communications) originate. Examinations of this nature can lead to an understanding of the year-by-year unfolding of our habits. In fact, the apostle Paul on several occasions reflected on his past experiences of anger as he testified about how God had transformed his life (see Acts 22:3-21). We can easily surmise that we are not taught in the Scriptures to ignore the past; rather, we are to understand it so we will become freed from it.

Several years ago a reporter asked a well-known national politician to describe the chief traits that qualify a person to hold a public office. Wisely, the politician replied that the individual must have the necessary historical frame of reference to make decisions for the present generation. In personal growth, the same premise holds true. An understanding of self becomes complete when the "big picture" is in view. Without obsessively dwelling on the past, an individual can learn to appreciate the fact that our current struggles can be due in large part to the cumulative effect of prior teachings and perceptions.

That value in gaining a perspective on our past experiences and personal struggles is that the solutions to our most prominent current struggles involve examining such issues as one's foundation for self-security, one's basic philosophy of self-talk, one's style of motivating self toward excellence, and one's reasons for acting undesirably to negative input. Our current struggles have been years in the making. As we are patient, we can work a resolution in these areas.

Even though we may not be consciously aware of the full impact the past is having on the present, those old thoughts and impressions can wield a silent influence. Many crucial teachings are imprinted upon our impressionable minds before our minds are able to decipher the full meaning of events and experiences.

No past experience is ever truly lost or completely forgotten. There are many times when unlocking and examining hurts of the past can have positive effects for handling the present. Therefore, it is better to gain knowledge about one's self by reflecting on past experiences rather than assuming that the past will merely fade away and leave the present untouched.

Step 3: Identify the guiding thoughts and ideas that are at the base of your personal struggles.

Whether or not we are aware of it, each of us has a philosophy of life that guides our every action and reaction. That philosophy is shaped by innumerable teachings (both experiential and spoken) beginning in childhood, and it becomes refined in the adult years.

The reason many people hold to illogical and non-scriptural teachings is not necessarily because they genuinely want to live in error. Rather, it is because they have not been taught to directly confront their guiding philosophies in a manner that causes them to deeply think through the ideas that truly bring peace of mind. Making true peace with our emotions must include a process of confronting the thinking that underlies our feelings.

Real transformation within cannot occur until we are able to confront the deepest inner thoughts that are associated with the outer problems and make the necessary mental adjustments.

Getting past the external behaviors and emotional expressions to underlying thoughts and beliefs requires that we have an understanding of the circumstances that create the emotions we struggle with. It assumes that we are able to "read the warnings" that are a part of our personal struggles. After we comprehend what our basic struggles are and know when they occur, we are then able to move to the stage of identifying and interpreting the thoughts that are associated with those struggles.

Gerald had made significant progress by acknowledging that his depression had elements of each of the five basic emotional struggles as well as a deficiency of love in his background. He focused specifically on the easily harbored feelings of inferiority and guilt that contributed most significantly to his problems.

When we identified those particular issues, he felt a sense of relief, because he was finally putting his finger on the factors leading to his long-standing bout with depression. He now realized the underlying problems. Our next step was to examine the thoughts that were dominating his mental processes.

We focused on the thoughts associated with deficient love needs and inferiority feelings and discovered that his mind had settled on inappropriate ideas of personal worth. His reasoning was that he could gain self-worth only as significant people would applaud him and extol his virtue.

As we uncovered those thoughts, we compared them to truths found in God's Word. Psalm 8:4-5 tells us that we have unmerited value to God. Romans 5:8 teaches that even in our most sinful condition God shows His love for us by offering salvation in the Person of Jesus Christ.

By contemplating those timeless, scriptural truths, Gerald was able to regain a sense of self-worth in spite of the insinuations of others. He recognized that God had given him His stamp of approval. He began to worry less about the amount of love and affirmation he received from humans because he knew he was loved by God.

Changing problematic thought patterns into Bible-centered thought patterns requires that we make the assumption that what God declares in His Word is indeed infallible. We do not go to the Bible merely to glean a few "feel good" statements that will lift us from lowly feelings. Rather, we assume that the Bible is a divinely inspired book that reveals the absolute truths that come directly from the mind of God. We can believe that because God does not desire that His created beings suffer in life-styles of aimlessness. He has given us the answers for our struggles.

By examining the thought patterns associated with human problems and making adjustments in our guiding thoughts, we underscore the deep conviction that transformation involves more than just making some "how to" adjustments in outer behaviors.

To change our outer behaviors without adjusting our inner style of thought is like repairing a sputtering car by giving it a paint job. No matter how dressed up it looks on the outside, the inner parts will still have problems when the car attempts to move on the highway. The person seeking true transformation must be one who is willing to overhaul even the innermost beliefs that propel self to action.

When the Bible's truths are contemplated, the task of switching from one system of thinking to the biblical system is not easy or automatic. Learning a new set of guiding principles can be as difficult as learning a foreign language. And even when the new language is successfully integrated into one's speech, the individual still thinks predominantly in the native language.

Learning a new language can take years. In the same way, new mental processes integrated into one's life-style can take several years to become first nature. Daily concentration for long periods of time is essential for successful integration.

As with identifying the underlying issues and examining background influences, the step of analyzing the guiding thoughts is not done on a one-time basis. Because the process of self-examination will bring many issues into the open, it is important to continually search for the thoughts that are in need of confrontation. The step of identifying the inner thoughts must be repeated frequently.

It is in this time of confrontation of inner thoughts that the successful outcome of true personal growth hinges. It can open our eyes to previously unattended blind spots, because there is no behavior or emotional expression that does not in some way reveal a truth about the inner self. We may not necessarily be aware of all that our emotions and behaviors communicate, but that does not negate the fact that they always carry inherent messages. The insightful individual will be one who will seek to look beyond the external to discern the internal meaning.

Step 4: Recognize how your struggles feed on each other.

Curt was a divorced, middle-aged man who sought counseling because of his inability to maintain satisfactory, close relationships. He had tried to date several women in the six years after his divorce, but each relationship broke off in a distasteful ending.

As Curt attempted to identify the foundations of his struggles, the only real problem he could identify was "being too critical." As Curt investigated the underlying causes of his criticisms, he discovered many interesting facts. For example, his critical nature was linked to continuing struggles with impatient anger. That led to the discovery that his anger had roots in his struggles with his self-image and feelings of inferiority.

Because anger and inferiority are preceded by unresolved loneliness and fears, I challenged Curt to recognize some of his other unnoticed struggles of fear of rejection and differentness, which actually propelled him to be critical in his futile attempt to bring conformity into his world.

In addition to what Curt had discovered for himself, he had a hidden sense of pride that fed his desire to be in control. That resulted in a non-accepting, imperative style of communication that pushed people away from him.

To complete this self-understanding step, it is helpful to note how underlying factors and problems relate to each other. As we understand the interrelationships of those problems, we are able to better coordinate our solutions.

In Curt's case, in order to be more kindhearted, he knew he needed to be mindful of his position in Christ and his need to let go of the controls, to communicate in a more free and accepting way, and to be less fearful of the evaluations of others.

Personal transformation can take place only as there is a broad-based comprehension of the aspects of our personality. And change is not likely to occur until we have a healthy respect for the complexities of our human frailities.

Step 5: Develop a growth strategy that converts inward changes to outward changes in your behavior and communication.

Whereas the main thrust of personal growth is to examine and restructure one's guiding thoughts, attitudes, and beliefs, there must be some external changes that indicate that the inner changes are real. In fact, we can assume that an inner transformation has not occurred in a significant way until some major differences in outer behavior occur.

That is consistent with Matthew 7:20, which tells us that people are known by their fruits. In many respects, the task of outlining our proper outer behavior is the easiest part of the growth process. Most of us are already aware of what we "should" be doing before we begin examining our thoughts and emotions. For example, a complaining person has no trouble recognizing that it is better to be more assertive. A shy person is aware of that fact.

The one factor that causes our behavior efforts to succeed or fail is the presence or lack of insight. For this reason it is beneficial to examine the inner meanings of our struggles before making grand plans to change behaviors. As correct mental processes become established, the desire and ability to persistently do what is right follows naturally.

Changed behavior does not come from having a good how-to formula, it comes from having a mind that is awakened to the need for yielding one's guiding thoughts to God's direction.

Nancy was a single woman in her early thirties who had been involved in a year-long affair with a married man. She realized that the affair was destroying the quality of her life and that she needed to break it off. But for some reason she seemed so addicted to the man that she could not let go.

An examination of the underlying causes for her actions turned up a background of insufficient love experiences in her home.

Although her parents were pleasant, Nancy had not felt satisfied in the realm of being loved. Often she felt that her father was so busy with his many projects that she was not high on his priority list. Nancy perceived that she would be loved by her mother only if she performed "properly."

Subconsciously, Nancy had set out in her adult life to find someone to love her just for who she was. She had convinced herself that she could feel content only if she could find the right person who would ascribe to her the worth and value she so longed for.

Unfortunately, when Mr. Right showed up, he was a married man. But aching to be loved, Nancy went against her best judgment and became romantically involved with him.

Nancy discovered through self-understanding that her dependency was born of an inability to resolve her loneliness. As we examined her background more closely, we also discovered a timidness that caused her to hold inwardly her assertiveness. That in turn created repressed anger that caused her to rebel against her moral upbringing and knowingly become involved in wrong behavior.

Nancy also found that she was prone to mystical thinking patterns, which led her to assume that a perfect relationship was "out there" waiting for her to claim. Those factors contributed to a mind-set that assumed a negative posture toward self, harbored rebellious thoughts toward God, and clung to an idealistic notion of contentment that could be gained in human love relationships.

When Nancy realized how poorly that mind-set matched up with teachings from Scripture, she made strong efforts to commit her life to God, to focus on His thoughts of the worth of the individual, His desire and ability to fellowship with her, and His reasons for asking that we live morally.

As Nancy's mind became more attuned to God's leadership, she knew that she would have to stop the affair so she could claim the inner peace that God so freely offered her.

Nancy found that her ability to stick to the game plan of spiritual living was possible after she had come to a well-rounded understanding of who she was.

A key point to underscore is that a growing individual cannot expect someone else to assume the final responsibility for the solutions of his or her problems. Whereas others may toss out some "what if" suggestions, it is preferable that any structural change in one's life result from personal choice. This is preferable for two reasons:

1. We need to have the satisfaction of knowing that the decision to change is based on free-will decisions. This enhances our level of self-esteem and sense of responsibility for implementing proper solutions.

2. We become less dependent upon others and develop more incentive to reasoning that is focused on God's direction.

As might be expected, the step of making plans for behavior changes is not a one-time event. As the various factors and stages in the growth process are contemplated, we need to constantly ask the question, How do these insights apply to my life-style?

The steps described in this chapter are designed to illustrate how we can know ourselves. Too often we develop a lack of awareness of who we are because we have not been challenged to think about the meanings of our emotional expressions, the reasons we do what we do, and the thoughts to which we give prominence. It is only as we develop an awareness of our real self that true personal growth can occur.